ORACLE PERFORMANCE TUNING ADVICE

By
Asim Chowdhury, Technical Architect & Designer

Foreword By
Arnab Bhattacharya, Associate Professor, Dept. of Computer Science and Engineering, **Indian Institute of Technology, Kanpur**, India

FOREWORD

Databases are ubiquitous. Since most databases in the world run on relational
Systems of which Oracle holds a primary position, the book is extremely timely
And useful. It gives key insights into how to get the best out from a working
Oracle system, and contains numerous examples to highlight the different cases.

The author, Asim Chowdhury, has a lot of experience in the field, especially in
Handling Oracle database systems. His multiple books prove that he is a
Successful author as well.

In sum, this is a book that every Oracle practitioner would love to have a copy.

Arnab Bhattacharya, Associate Professor, Dept. of Computer
Science and Engineering, **Indian Institute of Technology,
Kanpur**, India

PREFACE

I have one intention behind writing the book.

> ➤ Intention 2: Improve performance of oracle code by showcasing all possible alternative concepts present in database

This intention have arisen based on the burning need of database users I have come across throughout my career with roles like PL/SQL developers , Database Administrators, Designers, Data analysts, Performance tuning analysts, Architects, Students, Professors, Interviewees and any DBMS enthusiast or aspirant for oracle certification. Some of these had extensive experience in what they do and have influenced me writing this book.

This book will teach you how you can tune your database application by refactoring your code. Also it provides advices on tuning approach.

The audience of this book would like to cover multiple versions of Oracle and the features it offers. Seeking the best approach for a challenge has not been easy in past as it required a large investment of time and effort to go through the vast amount of documentation. This 135 pages book facilitates that investment, by exploring and churning the vast archives of oracle documentation and producing the output in a nutshell which otherwise readers would need to spend time on. Will appreciate if you can give your feedback in amazon, createspace or any online portal or reach me author.asim@gmail.com

-Author

ACKNOWLEDGEMENT

I would like to thank Stéphane Faroult (author of many Oracle books) who has been guiding me throughout the process. I am inspired by Tom Kyte (man behind asktom.com), Richard Foote (Oracle index specialist), Burleson consulting, Greg Doench (Pearson USA), Steven Feuerstein, I am indebted a lot to them.

My thanks go to Anish Joseph, Nag, Bala, Amit Kumar, Abhisek Kumar, Shakti panday, Vishal Jain, Amit Joshi, Amit Chitnis, Avinash Chinchwadkar, Mohsin Hashmi, Venkat, Baskar, Pankaj, Pratap, Deepak, Rashni, Vikash, Swapan, Sumanta and all my colleagues and friends from for their encouraging words. Apologies for not being able to mention the many other names.

I would like to convey my sincere thanks to my friend Arnab Bhattacharya (Professor of IIT KANPUR Computer Science) for his encouragement and for writing the foreword for this book.

My thanks go to my Father Chittaranjan Chowdhury and mother Shephali Chowdhury who taught me how to be simple but think big.

Also my thanks go to my father in-law R.N. Bhui and mother in-law Jharna Bhui for their constant encouragement.

My thanks go to my uncle Ajoy Kar (Professor of Heriot Watt University, Edinburgh) for his encouragement of my work.

My thanks go to my wife Sutapa Chowdhury who sacrificed her successful career in IT industry to take care of our lovely Aditi and give me more space to concentrate on the work for this book. My wife is my guiding star.

My biggest thanks go to my little daughter Aditi Chowdhury who sacrificed her playtime with me because of my busy involvement with this book, she also constantly asked about the progress and her simple enquiries touched a chord in such a way that it gave me the boost I needed to finish the gigantic task of writing this book.

My deep gratitude to Maa Anandamayee and Bashistha maharaja for the divine blessings.

And finally my thanks go to GOD for His constant blessings without which it is impossible to pursue this task. This book is dedicated to LORD Krishna and Maa Anandamayee.

-Author

Table of Contents:

Index scan improve performance of a query, here we will compare 2 approaches:

Approach 1: Normal Index Scan

This scan will happen if a predicate (where clause) refer to one of the column in an index. This scan will get the rowids from index and get the data from table quickly. This can reads the one index block at a time in contrast to FAST FULL INDEX SCAN which reads multiple index block at a time.

Approach 2: Fast Full Index Scan

FAST FULL INDEX SCAN, reads all the index blocks instead of the table blocks. This scan happens only when you are accessing table columns which are part of a concatenated index. This scan uses multiblock IO and hence perform very fast.

This scan is useful for reducing the numbers of logical reads by not accessing the table at all and hence is also named "INDEX ONLY SCAN". To take advantage of this SCAN it is sometimes necessary to add an extra column to an existing index.

Using EXPLAIN PLAN command you can check whether <u>fast full index scan</u> happen.

```
Explain plan FOR SELECT * FROM (TABLE_NAME);
SELECT plan_table_output
FROM TABLE(dbms_xplan.display('plan_table',NULL,'serial'));
```

Note DBMS_XPLAN.DISPLAY function provides four levels of output based on the third parameter:

BASIC:
```
SELECT plan_table_output
FROM TABLE(dbms_xplan.display('plan_table',NULL,'BASIC'));

| Id  | Operation      | Name        |
------------------------------------------
```

TYPICAL (default):
```
SELECT plan_table_output
FROM TABLE(dbms_xplan.display('plan_table',NULL,'TYPICAL'));
-----------------------------------------------------------------------
| Id  | Operation      | Name        | Rows  | Bytes | Cost (%CPU)| Time     |
-----------------------------------------------------------------------
```

SERIAL:
```
SELECT plan_table_output
FROM TABLE(dbms_xplan.display('plan_table',NULL,'SERIAL'));
-----------------------------------------------------------------------
| Id  | Operation      | Name        | Rows  | Bytes | Cost (%CPU)| Time     |
-----------------------------------------------------------------------
```

ALL:
```
SELECT plan_table_output
FROM TABLE(dbms_xplan.display('plan_table',NULL,'ALL'));
```

```
-----------------------------------------------------------------------
| Id | Operation       | Name    | Rows | Bytes | Cost (%CPU)| Time     |
-----------------------------------------------------------------------
```

Query Block Name / Object Alias (identified by operation id):

Column Projection Information (identified by operation id):

Column Projection information contains which predicate is executed first and which order.

Example how "fast full index scan" perform better than "normal index scan":

Without touching or accessing the data from a table you can retrieve the data from oracle index tree. This method is called "INDEX FAST FULL SCAN" or "INDEX ONLY SCAN"

Oracle implements this concept in the form of Index organized Table (IOT).
However without IOT you can also use Index only scan and get great performance improvement.

Using "**index only scan**", Oracle does not need to access the table because all the information is present in the index tree. To achieve this you need to build a super index on the columns from "**select list**" and the columns from "**where clause**".

However some catches:
> Index only scan is improved if the table has low clustering factor.
> High clustering factor means table data is not sequenced. If the table data has high clustering factor, then index only scan performance benefit is almost nominal and not recommended.
> If you add any extra column in "select clause" or in "where clause" then index only scan does not happen and it takes different execution plan based on many factors at that point of SCN.

Here is one example query which took 5 minute to execute and required to be tuned.

```
SELECT *
  FROM (  SELECT *
            FROM XX_V m
          WHERE m.X = 'LDN' AND m.Y = 'FIN'
        ORDER BY m.q1, m.q2, m.q3)
WHERE ROWNUM < 2502;
```

Few points about the query:
> The view in the query is based on some other views
> The view in the query uses function **f1**:
```
CREATE OR REPLACE
FUNCTION f1(p_in IN NUMBER)
  RETURN VARCHAR2
  AS
  language java name
  'com.xx.utility.rad50ToString(java.math.BigDecimal) return java.lang.String';
```
> The underlying table has all the suitable indexes and primary key in place properly. There is a unique concatenated index on "q1, q2, q3" columns.

➢ This query is used in the GUI for different screens and the response time is very slow. It takes more than 5 min for 1 million data in the underlying tables.

➢ The throughput is a benchmark and extraordinary, it process more than 5000 records per seconds.

Now the challenge is to improve the response time without sacrificing the throughput....

Using materialized view instead of view you can we see a **600% improve in response time**, but the throughput is dropped significantly.

The final solution for this is as below
1. Refactor the query using fast full index only scan (by refactoring the query) instead of normal index scan
2. Use deterministic keyword for the existing function which will internally use the pre-computed result and will be faster

The refactor query looks as below:
```
SELECT *
    FROM XX_V
    WHERE      (q1, q2, q3) IN (SELECT q1, q2, q3
                                    FROM (  SELECT q1, q2, q3
                                            FROM XX_V m
                                            WHERE m.X = 'LDN' AND m.Y = 'FIN'
                                        ORDER BY m.q1, m.q2, m.q3)
                                WHERE ROWNUM < 2502)
        AND X = 'LDN'
        AND Y = 'FIN'
ORDER BY q1, q2, q3;
```

Note instead of accessing all the table columns you select only q1, q2 and q3 column and hence invoke the "INDEX ONLY SCAN" and improve performance.

And the function is rewritten as below using DETERMINISTIC keyword:

```
CREATE OR REPLACE
FUNCTION f1(p_in IN NUMBER)
 RETURN VARCHAR2
 DETERMINISTIC
 AS
 language java name
 'com.xx.utility.rad50ToString(java.math.BigDecimal) return java.lang.String';
```

The **DETERMINISTIC** option helps the optimizer avoid redundant function calls. If a stored function was called previously with the same arguments, the optimizer can select to use the previous result.

The number of distinct values of "**P_IN**" argument which are passed to the function is only 20 and it returns **20** distinct java.lang.string but this function is used in a view which returns millions of records and hence the function computes the same 20 return value millions of times. However by means of **DETERMINISTIC** keyword you can use the pre computed 20 return values from the function and improve the performance of the view call significantly.
With both these changes the response time come down from 5 minutes to 3 seconds.

Index Join scan happens when <u>all the data retrieved</u> is from a combination of index columns. Here you can see all the data is present in an index columns and hence table access is avoided.
You can force an "index join" using hint /*+ INDEX_JOIN (table_name idx1 idx2) */

Individual index scan: If you have more than one index on different columns then oracle uses individual indexes separately and then merge the results from independent index scans.

Index join scan is very useful in high volume SQL where there is potential table lookup.
E.g.

```
CREATE TABLE apps_shop
  (
    app_id     NUMBER,
    shop_id    NUMBER,
    region     VARCHAR2(10),
    shop_desc  VARCHAR2(20),
    app_desc   VARCHAR2(20),
    status     VARCHAR2(1)
  );
CREATE INDEX apps_shop_idx on apps_shop(shop_id);
CREATE INDEX apps_region_idx on apps_shop(region);
```

Insert millions of records and then analyze the table/index.

Problem (Uses individual index scan):
Now you have a query which takes huge time:

```
SELECT COUNT(*) FROM apps_shop WHERE shop_id=2345 and region='ASIA';
```

This takes huge time because oracle will have index range scan on "shop_id" and "region" individually and then merge the results from independent index scans.

However if you can scan the index together to get the required data it will be quick because both the filter criteria together return only handful of rows. So to achieve the fast response time we have 2 solutions:

Solution 1:
Drop the individual indexes and create a concatenated index as below:

```
CREATE INDEX apps_shop_region_idx on apps_shop(shop_id,region);
```

Solution 2:
Use INDEX_JOIN hints which will force the optimizer to use both the indexes together and thus avoid table access as all the information are available in the index columns "shop_id" and "region"

```
SELECT /*+ INDEX_JOIN(apps_shop apps_shop_idx apps_region_idx) */ COUNT(*)
FROM apps_shop WHERE shop_id=2345 and region='ASIA';
```

Oracle does not store null value in B-tree index and hence when you query for null column values, an index is not used even if there is an index on that column. This degrade the performance of your application.

There are two ways to store null in B-tree index by creating special index on null column to improve performance:

Approach 1:
Create index on expression
```
CREATE INDEX idx1 ON table_name
  (null_column,-999
  );
```
Now if you have query as below the index will be used:
```
SELECT * FROM table_name WHERE null_column IS NULL;
```

Approach 2:
Create function based index on NVL function
```
CREATE INDEX idx2 ON table_name
  (NVL (null_column,-888)
  );
```
Now if you have query as below the index will be used:
```
SELECT * FROM table_name WHERE NVL (null_column,-888) =<SOME VALUE>;
```

Here we will discuss how to minimize processing time by using DISTINCT in appropriate place.

Distinct after applying a function
You can eliminate unnecessary processing time by using DISTINCT appropriately.
E.g. instead of using
```
SELECT DISTINCT user_def_fun (name) FROM TABLE_NAME;
```

In this approach you are applying **user_def_fun** function on all the records and hence increasing the processing time as you are unnecessarily letting the function to execute on duplicate records.

Distinct before applying a function

```
SELECT user_def_fun (name) FROM
  (SELECT DISTINCT name FROM TABLE_NAME
  );
```

In this approach you are applying **user_def_fun** function only on the distinct records and not on all the records and hence reducing the processing time and improving performance.

Note: First you have to create the user defined function "user_def_fun". However the concept can be tried using oracle defined function like "UPPER", "LOWER" etc. So just replace "user_def_fun" by "UPPER" in the above example.

Here we will discuss different approaches for improving the performance of SQL query and role of different statistics including function based statistics for enhanced performance.

Statistics consist of row density, clustering factor, and number of distinct values, smallest, largest value, data distribution (column histogram) and presence of NULL etc. These statistics are used by optimizer to estimate the selectivity of WHERE clause predicates.

Statistics for a table/index is generated as below:
```
Analyze TABLE Test11 compute statistics;

Analyze INDEX test11_f_count_occurances_idx compute statistics;
```

However analyze command is supported for backward compatibility, you can instead use DBMS_STATS:

```
EXEC DBMS_STATS.gather_table_stats('U1', 'TEST11');
EXEC DBMS_STATS.gather_index_stats('U1', 'TEST11_F_COUNT_OCCURANCES_IDX');
```

If you would like to delete the stats use:
```
EXEC DBMS_STATS.delete_table_stats('U1', 'TEST11');
```

Without statistics optimizer has no information on how to derive the best execution plan and end up in giving sub-optimal plan and degrade performance.

Also you must gather statistics for PL/SQL functions if they are used in SQL predicate. **Without function statistics** Oracle executes the query based on the order in which the predicate conditions appears in the "where" clause. So if you have less selective predicate function before the most selective predicate in your query then Oracle, in the absence of statistics, executes in the same order and hence performs slower. However if you gather statistics then Oracle will internally execute the most selective predicate before it executes the less selective predicates and this results in improved performance.

Note statistics are used not only for deciding if Index/full table scan will be used but used for deciding selective predicate order in where clause, choosing appropriate JOIN methods.
Function statistics can be generated using command:
```
Associate statistics
WITH FUNCTIONS <FUNCTION name> DEFAULT selectivity 50;
```

Statistics generated using Associate statistics are "**default statistics**" and used only to help CBO to order the functions based on selectivity when used in SQL predicates.
To gather stats for table the command:
```
Analyze TABLE <TABLE name> compute statistics;
```

Again when you have multiple columns of the same table or you have expression (e.g. some oracle/user defined function) used in the predicate, then it is not possible for CBO to derive the selectivity of the column group or selectivity of the expression against another table column predicate using normal statistics. However using "**Extended Statistics**" it is possible to get the selectivity of group of columns and expressions. Also extended statistics has the added benefit that a function based index can be used not only in predicate clause but also in group by and having clause.

Extended statistics can be generated explicitly and implicitly as below:
Explicitly generated extended statistics:

```
DECLARE
  l_extend_stat VARCHAR2(30);
BEGIN
  l_extend_stat := DBMS_STATS.create_extended_stats
                    (ownname => 'HR',
                     tabname => 'EMPLOYEES',
                     extension => '(LOWER(first_name))'
                     );
   --For group of columns you can use extension=>'(column1,column2)'
END;
/
```

Implicitly generated extended statistics:

```
EXEC dbms_stats.gather_table_stats
                ('HR','EMPLOYEES',
                  method_opt=>'for columns (UPPER(first_name))'
                );
```

Note extended stats are based on HASH function and hence they **work only with predicates based on equality** and do not work if you use <>, <, > and "BETWEEN" operators. Extended stats are used in DISTINCT operator also from 11gR2 onwards.

The difference between "Default statistics" and "Extended statistics" are
  - ○ "Default Statistics" has fixed selectivity whereas for "Extended Statistics" selectivity is dynamic
  - ○ "Default Statistics" is used only for predicate ordering of function in SQL "where" clause however "Extended Statistics" is used not only for predicate ordering but for making the function based index used in "Group by" and "Order by" clauses.

So if you have extended statistics you do not need default statistics.
You can view the column group or expression extended statistics has been generated for using the following query:
```
SELECT * FROM dba_stat_extensions WHERE owner='HR';
```

Advice 6: Refactoring a code OR no refactoring

Refactoring is a process of restructuring existing code without changing the behaviour of the code. Refactoring helps immensely to improve the response time of an application.

Without refactoring you have to pay the penalty in terms of poor response time.

In a nutshell presenting few ways you can refactor your code (Details you learn in subsequent advice in this book)

  - ➤ Use WITH clause factoring
  - ➤ Use Analytic function
  - ➤ Use "UNION" instead of "OR" operator.
  - ➤ Use CASE/DECODE statement
  - ➤ Use EXISTS instead of IN
  - ➤ Use proper datatype otherwise implicit conversion on the indexed column prevent the index to be used

- Declared variable and assignment should be in conformity otherwise internal type conversion degrade performance, e.g. "DECLARE a NUMBER :=1" will internally converted to "a :=1.0". So refactor you code to use "DECLARE a PLS_INTEGER :=1" or "DECLARE a NUMBER :=1.0".
- Refactor your code by means of using conditional $IF which will not only save memory by using the declared variable if it is required and also eliminate unnecessary code to be evaluated and improve performance
- Use fully qualified column reference in your query
- Avoid NOT IN as NOT IN does not allow an index to be used.
- Do not use "IS NULL" and "IS NOT NULL" on indexed column
- Do not apply a function on indexed column, if at all you need to use, create function based index
- Never do a calculation on indexed column
- Do not frequently commit in your code
- Use "WHEN" clause while creating TRIGGER to restrict it to be fired appropriately.
  "WHEN" clause used in a trigger restricts the trigger execution based on the condition mentioned in the "WHEN" clause. Note do not use ":" before **NEW/OLD** pseudo column in the "**WHEN**" clause.
  E.g.

```
CREATE OR REPLACE TRIGGER trig_check_tab_t before
    INSERT OR UPDATE ON check_tab_t FOR EACH row WHEN NEW.sal>10000
```

- Use "OUT NOCOPY", "IN OUT NOCOPY" in your subprogram parameter
- Use PLSQL_OPTIMIZE_LEVEL parameter to value 3 for program inlining
- Use bulk feature like "FORALL" "BULK COLLECT" to reduce context switch between engines.
- Using package cache the frequently used values in memory
- Using KEEP pool you can keep a table in memory
- Refactor the code to use one parse many execute by means of bind variables
- Save PGA memory by refactoring your code to use pragma serially_reusable. This may degrade performance as the package state is discarded as soon as the execution is over. So there is a trade-off between PGA memory requirement and performance and hence choose carefully.
- Use join instead of subquery
- Use WHERE clause filtering before using HAVING clause filtering
- Use DISTINCT clause appropriately to reduce the work.
- Use pipeline table function which works like "FIRST_ROW hint" and improve performance for OLTP application.
- Use "Indices of" clause for sparse collection
- Use index by table for frequently used lookup tables as index by table store the data in PGA as memory access is 1000 time faster than disk access
- Use of Oracle hints (Hint is a suggestion to the optimizer)
  E.g.

```
SELECT /*+ NL_SJ */   --Nested loop semi join
SELECT /*+ HASH_SJ */ --Hash semi join
SELECT /*+ FULL(e) CACHE(e) */ COUNT(*) FROM EMP e;
--This puts the result of full table scan in the most recently used end of LRU
```

Advice 7: Compression *OR* no compression

Compression of table/index decreases the storage space and improve performance for index range scan/table scan as oracle has to scan less number of table/index block.
We will also look into oracle 12c Advanced Index compression while rebuilding or creating an index.

Without compression oracle has to incur the cost associated with scanning additional table/index blocks.

Compression was introduced in Oracle 8i where you can compress only index keys. Oracle 9i added compression for Tables but it can only be done while creating via direct load or CTAS or Insert with Append. Oracle 11g introduced advanced compression where you can create a table with **COMPRESS FOR OLTP**.

```
CREATE TABLE tabl
  (
    a NUMBER,
    b VARCHAR2 (30),
    c VARCHAR2 (20)
  )
  COMPRESS FOR OLTP;
```

Also you can compress a table after creation using Alter command. `ALTER TABLE tabl move COMPRESS;`
Run the following query **before** the alter command and **after** the ALTER command to see how much space is regained by compression. Compression not only saves space but any query against the table after compression has improved performance as the number of BLOCKs scanned is reduced dramatically.

```
SELECT segment_name,
  segment_type,
  blocks
FROM dba_segments
WHERE segment_name IN ('TAB1');
```

Similarly while creating or rebuilding index you can use compression which allows us to store the index in fewer database blocks which not only save space but improve performance on large index range scan and index fast full scan.

```
ALTER INDEX index_name REBUILD ONLINE COMPRESS;
```

However one must be careful before compressing a particular index. If an index does not have lot of repeated data compression of index may lead to increase in storage space because of oracle internal mechanism of storing the index blocks.
You can see amount of space occupied by index (which can be run before and after compression):

```
SELECT index_name,
  leaf_blocks,--This will provide the storage space of index
  compression
FROM user_indexes
WHERE table_name='TABLE_NAME';
```

However from **Oracle 12c** onwards you need not worry whether compression will lead to increase in storage space because oracle 12c has introduced "**Advanced Index compression**" which will always decrease the storage space and improve performance for index range scan. This advanced feature is available only in enterprise edition.

In order to use "**Advanced Index compression**" just use the keyword "compress advanced low" while creating/rebuilding the index.

```
ALTER INDEX index_name REBUILD COMPRESS ADVANCED LOW;
```

After compressing an index using this option you can run the above "SELECT" query and will see that the leaf_blocks value is significantly lesser.
Note: "Advanced Index compression" does not work on unique single-column indexes.

Normalization is a process of breaking a relation (table) into smaller relation (table) with a view to reduce redundant data and create appropriate structure. There are mainly 3 normal forms.

1NF: Here all the attributes (columns) values of a **table** are atomic (indivisible).
>   This normal form implements the following rules:
> ➢ Eliminate repeating groups in a table.
> ➢ For each set of related data create a table

The disadvantage of 1NF are:
> ➢ Redundant data
> ➢ You cannot remove a particular row as by deleting a row, you lose other important attribute values. E.g. if you remove employee rows from EMPLOYEE table (1NF) you lose department details.
> ➢ You cannot add a new department until an employee joins the department.

2NF: This means a table is in 1NF and additionally all the non-key attributes (columns) are dependent on the primary key column. However two non-key attributes (columns) **may be dependent** on each other
The disadvantage of 2NF are:
> ➢ Redundant data (less than 1NF)
> ➢ You cannot independently modify one non key attribute value as it may have dependencies with other non-key attributes. E.g. if the designation of an employee changes in EMPLOYEE table (2NF) you must change the dependent non key attribute (column) also.

3NF: This means a table is in 2NF and two non-key attributes (columns) **cannot be dependent** on each other. The objective of 3NF is to remove data from a table that is not dependent on primary key and place them in another table.

The **objective** of **normalization** are:
> ➢ To reduce redundant data.
> ➢ To maintain data consistency
> ➢ Flexible design to maintain the data
> ➢ To maintain data integrity
> ➢ To maintain database security

The redundant data causes the following problems:
> ➢ If same data is kept in more than one table unnecessary space is used
> ➢ With duplicate data present in different tables, there is a chance of making mistake by updating only one set of data from one table instead of all the tables where the same duplicate data exists. This increases the cost of maintenance and risk of failure as data can be inconsistent across the system.

De-normalization is the process of storing redundant data to improve read performance of database at the expense of throughput. So there should be trade-off between response time and throughput when to use normalization and de-normalization.

Many times we **introduce redundancy** to a certain extent in a database to improve performance, in other words we de-normalize a table to reduce the cost of table JOINS to get data faster from a table without incurring the cost of JOINING multiple tables ("Joining" results in more I/O and CPU time). So there is a trade off in doing this. As a rule you normalize the data model however based on performance requirement you can sometime introduce limited redundancy to retrieve data faster and more efficiently.

One of the example of de-normalization is "Materialized view" which store redundant data but eliminates the need to join multiple tables and thus improve performance of materialized view. In fact we introduce limited redundancy in table level also to improve performance of critical queries.

Advice 9: Oracle FOR UPDATE *OR* FOR UPDATE SKIP LOCKED

FOR UPDATE:

In oracle when FOR UPDATE is used in one session for a set of rows then those rows are locked until a commit/rollback is issued. If another session uses FOR UPDATE clause for the same set of rows (or all the rows) then the session will wait for the rows to be unlocked.

Session 1:
```
SELECT * FROM emp WHERE employee_id=7369 FOR UPDATE;
```

Session 2:
```
SELECT * FROM emp FOR UPDATE;
```
This will simply wait till session 1 commit/rollback.

If you use NOWAIT clause it will comeout with error:
```
SELECT * FROM emp FOR UPDATE nowait;
```
ORA-00054: resource busy and acquire with NOWAIT specified or timeout expired

So the **problem** is you cannot work on other rows which are not locked by session 1.

Solution using FOR UPDATE SKIP LOCKED:

Oracle 11g introduced FOR UPDATE SKIP LOCKED clause which will let you work on the records which are not locked by any other sessions.

Session 1:
```
SELECT * FROM emp WHERE employee_id=7369 FOR UPDATE;
```

Session 2:
```
SELECT * FROM emp FOR UPDATE skip locked;
```

This will return all the rows except employee_id=7369 which is locked by **session 1**.

DDL_LOCK_TIMEOUT:

In Oracle, running "ALTER" statement to add or modify table column causes below error
ORA-00054: resource busy and acquire with NOWAIT specified or timeout expired
So DBA has to try the "ALTER" command repeatedly <u>to get the exclusive **lock**</u>.

However in Oracle 11g you can set DDL_LOCK_TIMEOUT to certain value and hence the "ALTER" command will wait for that specified period (For this case 30 seconds) before it fails with ORA-00054

```
ALTER SESSION SET DDL_LOCK_TIMEOUT=30;
```

If the DML is committed within 30 seconds then the ALTER command will be successful.

Here we will discuss with a short example how to use "LIKE" operator so that index is used.

When using LIKE operator in a query and you want the index to be used then the wildcard (%) cannot be used as a predicate. The wildcard (%) can be used in the middle or end of the string.
e.g.

```
SELECT * FROM TABLE_NAME WHERE name LIKE '%FAR%' --will NOT use an INDEX
SELECT * from TABLE_NAME where name like 'FAR%'  --will use INDEX
```

Materialized view is a database object that contain the results of a query. Unlike a standard view which does not store data, a materialized view stores data similar to physical tables. This provides a fast response by pre-computing and storing aggregated information. The only disadvantage is that a materialized view may be out of sync because of change in underlying data in the base tables. However using fast refresh you can keep mview always in sync with base tables.
E.g. syntax

```
CREATE MATERIALIZED VIEW Mview_name BUILD
IMMEDIATE | DEFFERED | ON PREBUILT TABLE REFRESH COMPLETE | FAST
| FORCE ON COMMIT | ON DEMAND | START WITH ENABLE QUERY REWRITE
AS
  (SELECT * FROM tabl WHERE ....
  );
```

Result Cache is a mechanism by which oracle checks if the result of your query resides in cache (This is applicable for cross sessions). If the result is present oracle skip the execution step and provides the result directly from cache.
Sql result cache can be implemented using result_cache hint.

Here we will discuss how to get the result of a query stored in permanent form but always provide the latest data by means of RESULT_CACHE.

Materialized view is a database object which physically stores the pre-joined complex views and pre-computed result of a complex query. So when user tries to select from the mview, Oracle does not re-execute the underlying query but directly displays the pre-computed results from the stored mview. The mview is refreshed only then the underlying query is re-executed. So data in the mview is as accurate as the point of time of refresh but not accurate at the current point of time. So when taking a decision to use mview you must consider whether the mview being out of sync for certain period will impact the business. [Please note by using Automatic fast refresh of materialized views we can resolve the out of sync data issue, however it impacts throughput of application as it has to write into mview log on each commit and hence is very expensive]

In Oracle 11g we can overcome the issue of out of sync data in materialized view by means of "**Result_cache**" hint.
Also by using "**Result_cache**" hints you avoid the overhead of setting up and maintaining a materialized view.

```
SELECT /*+ result_cache */
  a.*.b.* FROM tab1, tab2 WHERE a.id=b.id;
```

So here when the query is executed for the 1st time it stores the result in a result cache similar to storing pre-computed/pre-joined query result and hence subsequent execution will use the result cache instead of re-executing the query.
However there is another advantage of using result cache: it will automatically refresh the result cache when the underlying base table's data are modified. So this result into getting accurate data as of current point of time with high response time without impacting throughput.

Advice 13: PL/SQL code optimization by "inlining" using PLSQL_OPTIMIZE_LEVEL 3 OR PRAGMA INLINE OR 12c WITH clause OR 12c PRAGMA UDF

Here we will explore different ways to **inline**/rearrange the subprogram by the PL/SQL compiler during compilation time to get better performance.

Subprogram inlining is the process by which oracle internally replaces the stored program code in the calling program **during compilation**. Since the stored code (procedure/function) is in the main code (INLINE) the extra time and context switching for calling the program from oracle server is eliminated and this in turn improve performance for oracle PL/SQL code execution.

Here are different ways of Inlining subprogram:

Approach 1: <u>By using PRAGMA INLINE compiler directive</u>

```
SQL> CREATE OR REPLACE PROCEDURE normal_p(name IN OUT VARCHAR2)
  2  IS
  3       a VARCHAR2(100);
  4  BEGIN
  5       a :=lower(name);
  6  END normal_p;
  7  /
```

Now call "normal_p" procedure by making this procedure inline using pragma inside function "inline_demo_step"

```
SQL> CREATE OR REPLACE FUNCTION inline_demo_step RETURN NUMBER
  2  IS
  3      b VARCHAR2(100);
  4  BEGIN
  5      PRAGMA INLINE('normal_p','YES');
  6      FOR i IN (SELECT employee_name FROM emp) LOOP
  7          b :=i.employee_name;
  8          normal_p(b);
  9          DBMS_OUTPUT.PUT_LINE('name is:'||b);
 10      END LOOP;
 11      RETURN 1;
 12  END inline_demo_step;
 13  /
```

Now you can execute the function:

```
SQL> set serveroutput on
SQL> select inline_demo_step from dual;

INLINE_DEMO_STEP
----------------
               1

name is:SMITH
name is:ALLEN
name is:WARD
name is:JONES
name is:MARTIN
name is:BLAKE
name is:CLARK
name is:SCOTT
name is:KING
name is:TURNER
name is:ADAMS
name is:JAMES
name is:FORD
name is:MILLER
```

So by using this Pragma, the optimizer will internally substitute the procedure code for inline_p and eliminate the overhead of extra call to server and enhance performance.

Please note we can use this pragma from Oracle 11g onward.

Approach 2: By using 12c WITH clause

In 12c you can INLINE function/procedure using "**WITH**" clause. You can have faster running procedure or function if they are defined and declared inside "WITH" clause of SQL statement.

In PL/SQL if you want call/execute a procedure or function having a "WITH" clause, you must use dynamic sql.

The scenario in approach 1, can be implemented using 12c WITH clause as below:

(**Note:** PL/SQL function using "WITH clause" does not work in some version of **SQLDEVELOPER**, so you must use sql*plus in case it does not work in your SQLDEVELOPER version for trying out all the examples given here.
)

```
SQL> SET serveroutput ON
SQL> WITH PROCEDURE normal_p(name IN OUT VARCHAR2) IS a VARCHAR2(100);
  2    BEGIN
  3      a :=lower(name);
  4    END;
  5    FUNCTION inline_demo_step
  6      RETURN VARCHAR2
  7    IS
  8      b VARCHAR2(100);
  9    BEGIN
 10      FOR i IN
 11      (SELECT employee_name FROM emp
 12      )
 13      LOOP
 14        b:=i.employee_name;
 15        normal_p(b);
 16        DBMS_OUTPUT.PUT_LINE('name is:'||b);
 17      END LOOP;
 18      RETURN 1;
 19    END;
 20    SELECT inline_demo_step FROM dual;
 21    /
```

The output is:

```
INLINE_DEMO_STEP
---------------------------------

1

name is:SMITH
name is:ALLEN
name is:WARD
name is:JONES
name is:MARTIN
name is:BLAKE
name is:CLARK
name is:SCOTT
name is:KING
name is:TURNER
name is:ADAMS
name is:JAMES
name is:FORD
name is:MILLER
```

Note: In order to call the WITH clause from subquery you must use WITH_PLSQL hint `/*+ WITH_PLSQL */`
You can use the WITH FUNCTION/PROCEDURE in update statement using `/*+ WITH_PLSQL */` operator. This operator is used like an oracle hints by embedding in UPDATE statement. If you do not use the operator then the statement will fail:

```
ORA-32034: unsupported use of WITH clause
```

Approach 3: By using 12c PRAGMA UDF

Here we will discuss compiler directive UDF to remove context switch between SQL and PL/SQL for function. This Pragma UDF is used to rearrange/inline a code for better performance.

SQL and PL/SQL has different memory representation and hence when a PL/SQL function is called from a select statement there are context switches between SQL and PL/SQL engines.
To resolve this Oracle 12c has introduced inlining using "WITH FUNCTION" clause which will invoke the function instantly in the SELECT statement with no context switching.
Also to resolve the context switching Oracle 12c has introduced "PRAGMA UDF". This is a compiler directive which states that the function is a "user defined function" and this function is used primarily in SQL select statement.

So the "WITH FUNCTION" and "PRAGMA UDF" similarity is that both are inlining the function and reduce the context switches between SQL and PL/SQL engines.

Difference between the two is:

"WITH FUNCTION" defines the PL/SQL subprogram **inside** the SQL statement.

"PRAGMA UDF"   defines the PL/SQL subprogram **outside** the SQL statement.

Converting a normal function to PRAGMA UDF function is the better approach because:

1. Using Pragma UDF you can make the code procedural and hence maintenance is easy and
   Less chance of making mistake
2. Get the advantage of inlining function which reduces context switches.
3. Moving from existing normal function to UDF function is fairly straightforward as against
   "**WITH FUNCTION**" clause which requires massive code changes where there is a function call in your application.

However if you are not worried about point **1 and 3** mentioned here then it is advisable to use "WITH FUNCTION" rather than "PRAGMA UDF" as I have seen "WITH FUNCTION" outperform "PRAGMA UDF" many times. In any case you must try all the approaches before finalizing your choice.

Both "**WITH FUNCTION**" and "**PRAGMA UDF**" method perform better than conventional function as long as these functions are called from SQL select statement. However if the "PRAGMA UDF" function is called from PL/SQL using direct call e.g. v1:=fun_pragma_udf (para1) then "PRAGMA UDF" method will drastically reduce the performance compared to a normal function. This is because Oracle "PRAGMA UDF" definition itself states the usage of this clause is beneficial only if the function is called from SQL SELECT.

```
SQL> CREATE OR REPLACE PROCEDURE normal_p(name IN OUT VARCHAR2)
  2  IS
  3  PRAGMA UDF;
  4      a VARCHAR2(100);
  5  BEGIN
  6      a :=lower(name);
  7  END normal_p;
  8  /
```

Now call this procedure directly from function "inline_demo_step".

```
SQL> CREATE OR REPLACE FUNCTION inline_demo_step RETURN NUMBER
  2  IS
  3      PRAGMA UDF;
  4      b VARCHAR2(100);
  5  BEGIN
  6      FOR i IN (SELECT employee_name FROM emp) LOOP
  7          b :=i.employee_name;
  8          normal_p(b);
  9          DBMS_OUTPUT.PUT_LINE('name is:'||b);
 10      END LOOP;
 11      RETURN 1;
 12  END inline_demo_step;
 13  /
```

Now you can execute the function:

```
SQL> set serveroutput on
SQL> select inline_demo_step from dual;

INLINE_DEMO_STEP
----------------
               1

name is:SMITH
name is:ALLEN
name is:WARD
name is:JONES
name is:MARTIN
name is:BLAKE
name is:CLARK
name is:SCOTT
name is:KING
name is:TURNER
name is:ADAMS
name is:JAMES
name is:FORD
name is:MILLER
```

Restriction of PRAGMA UDF

When IN or OUT parameter of a function is of data type "DATE" then UDF performs slowly
When the IN parameter data type (varchar2) has got any default value then UDF performs slowly.

Approach 4: By setting PLSQL_OPTIMIZE_LEVEL parameter to value 3

Since oracle 10g, PL/SQL code can be optimized during compilation time. This is done through optimizer setting PLSQL_OPTIMIZE_LEVEL to value 0, 1, 2 (2 is default) or 3.

The higher the value you set the more time it will take for the optimizer to compile the code but less time will be taken to execute the code.

PLSQL_OPTIMIZE_LEVEL =3 will enable PL/SQL inlining prior to compilation.

```
ALTER SESSION SET PLSQL_OPTIMIZE_LEVEL = 3;
```

So when we set it to 3 oracle will automatically try and inline/rearrange the subprogram at compile time, however sometimes oracle prefers not to inline the subprogram even if it is set to 3 because it believes it is undesirable. The default value of this parameter is 2.

When you have **PLSQL_OPTIMIZE_LEVEL=3** and still you want to avoid inlining for some specific subprogram, then you can use
PRAGMA INLINE (subprogram_name,'NO') to achieve that.

You can see the current optimization setting for procedure:
```
SELECT name,plsql_optimize_level
FROM USER_PLSQL_OBJECT_SETTINGS
WHERE upper(name)='PROC_FLEXIBLE_COMMIT';
```

Output:

NAME	PLSQL_OPTIMIZE_LEVEL
PROC_FLEXIBLE_COMMIT	2

26

Note: **PLSQL_OPTIMIZE_LEVEL=3** was introduced in 11g, however optimization level 0, 1, 2 was there in pre-11g.

So here are the suggestions in the order of best performance
→1st Try with SQL select if you can achieve the same functionality as the function.
→2nd Try a **function** using **Result cache or user**
→3rd Try with SQL select and "WITH FUNCTION" clause as per **approach 2**, if you are not worried about maintenance
    Cost and you are working with Oracle 12c release
→4th Use "PRAGMA UDF" and WITH CLAUSE together in your function as per **approach 2 &3**, if you are in oracle 12c
    Release
→5th Use "PRAGMA UDF" in your function as per **approach 3**, if you are in oracle 12c release
→6th Use PRGMA INLINE as per **approach 1** in your function if you are in oracle 11g or above.
→7th Use **PLSQL_OPTIMIZE_LEVEL=3** as per **approach 4**,if you are in oracle 10g and bove.
→8th Use conventional function

Note: This is just a suggestion, however before choosing any approach you must try all the options mentioned and accordingly take a call for your situations.

Advice 14: ROWID *OR* Unique key column for update

Update using unique key column:
In this approach for the unique key column it will find corresponding rowid and for that rowid it will update the record.

Update using ROWID:
In this approach you remove the step of finding ROWID and directly update the record

So when using "CURSOR FOR LOOP" or Normal cursor to update iteratively it is advisable to use ROWID instead of UNIQUE key column to update a record for better performance.
To achieve this you add ROWID in the SELECT clause of the CURSOR or in a normal "FOR LOOP" and in the update statement use "ROWID" in the filter clause instead of using UNIQUE key column employee_id.

Example of using ROWID instead of UNIQUE KEY:

```
BEGIN
  FOR i IN
  (SELECT employee_id,salary,job_id,rowid FROM employees
  )
  LOOP
    UPDATE employees
    SET salary =DECODE(i.job_id,'IT_PROG',i.salary*1.3,'IT_MGR',i.salary*1.2,i.salary*1.1)
    WHERE rowid=i.rowid;
  END LOOP;
END;
/
```

Here we will discuss how to reduce I/O by returning nested cursor from within a query.

Cursor expressions return nested cursor from within a query. The nested cursor is implicitly opened when the cursor expression is fetched from within a query.

So using cursor expression you can return normal data as well as complex parent-child data in a single query which results in reduced I/O and improved performance.

Normal cursor approach:

Let us take one example as to how it works without cursor expression:

```
SET serveroutput ON
BEGIN
  FOR i IN
  ( SELECT p.cust_id FROM dc_cust
  )
  LOOP
    dbms_output.put_line('parent is:'||i.cust_id);
    FOR j IN
    ( SELECT c.location_id FROM cust_loc c WHERE cust_id = i.cust_id
    )
    LOOP
      dbms_output.put_line('child is:'||j.location_id);    This query is executed for each cust_id
    END LOOP;
  END LOOP;
END;
/
```

The output:

```
anonymous block completed
parent is:110529
child is:22318
child is:36907        Child for the parent 110529
child is:54240
parent is:110606
child is:24
child is:2683         Child for the parent 110606
```

Note there is huge I/O involved to achieve this as in the second loop you execute the query for each record of first loop.

Cursor with cursor expression approach:

However using cursor expression you can do this with single query executed only once and produce the same result:

```
SET serveroutput ON
DECLARE
  l_dc_cust_id dc_cust.cust_id%TYPE;
  l_children SYS_REFCURSOR;
  l_loc_id dc_loc.location_id%TYPE;
  CURSOR c_cust_id_loc IS
    SELECT p.cust_id,CURSOR(SELECT c.location_id FROM dc_loc c WHERE c.cust_id = p.cust_id) occu_loc
    FROM dc_cust p;
BEGIN                        This is cursor expression
  OPEN c_cust_id_loc;
  LOOP
    FETCH c_cust_id_loc INTO l_dc_cust_id,l_children;
    EXIT WHEN c_cust_id_loc%NOTFOUND;
    DBMS_OUTPUT.put_line('Parent is: ' || l_parent);
    LOOP                            The cursor expression result is fetched into this nested cursor
      FETCH l_children INTO l_loc_id;       And this open the REF cursor implicitly
      EXIT WHEN l_children%NOTFOUND;
      DBMS_OUTPUT.put_line('Child is: ' || l_loc_id);
    END LOOP;
    CLOSE l_children;
  END LOOP;
  CLOSE c_cust_id_loc;
END;
/
```

So even if the coding is more in this approach, still it is advisable to use this because it **reduce I/O and improve performance.**

Advice 16: BULK DML using FORALL *OR* FORALL INDICES OF

Bulk DML is the process of modifying more than 1 record by incurring just 1 context switch between SQL and PL/SQL engine. Bulk DML is implemented using "FORALL" construct.

Approach 1: BULK DML using FORALL

Setup:
```
CREATE TABLE test_num(a number);
INSERT INTO test_num VALUES(10);
INSERT INTO test_num VALUES(20);
INSERT INTO test_num VALUES(30);
INSERT INTO test_num VALUES(40);
INSERT INTO test_num VALUES(50);
COMMIT;

CREATE TABLE test_num_copy(a number);
```

Run the code using FORALL to copy the data:

```
DECLARE
TYPE tl IS TABLE OF NUMBER INDEX BY binary_integer;
  v_tl tl;
BEGIN
  SELECT DISTINCT a bulk collect INTO v_tl FROM test_num;
  v_tl.delete(2);--This remove 2nd element
  FORALL i IN 1..v_tl.count
  INSERT INTO test_num_copy VALUES(v_tl(i));
END;
/
```

```
ORA-22160: element at index [2] does not exist
```

This fails because you have deleted 2nd element from the collection and then trying to INSERT into table test_num_copy all the rest of the element.

Solution:
You have to rearrange the element of the nested table which has become sparse because of some element deleted. This is done by copying all the remaining element into one more index by table as shown.

```
SET SERVEROUTPUT ON
DECLARE
TYPE tl IS TABLE OF NUMBER INDEX BY binary_integer;
  v_tl tl;
  v_non_sparse_tl tl;
  x BINARY_INTEGER;
BEGIN
  SELECT DISTINCT a bulk collect INTO v_tl FROM test_num;
  v_tl.delete(2);--This remove 2nd element
  x :=v_tl.FIRST;
  WHILE (x IS NOT NULL)
  LOOP
  v_non_sparse_tl(v_non_sparse_tl.COUNT+1) :=v_tl(x);
  x :=v_tl.next(x);
  END LOOP;
  FORALL k IN 1..v_non_sparse_tl.count
  INSERT INTO test_num_copy VALUES(v_non_sparse_tl(k));
END;
/
```

Approach 2: BULK DML using FORALL INDICES OF

"INDICES OF" clause let us iterate over <u>non-consecutive sparse collection</u> (which has got some deleted element in between) in a FORALL statement.
Solution:

```
DECLARE
TYPE tl IS TABLE OF NUMBER INDEX BY binary_integer;
  v_tl tl;
BEGIN
  SELECT DISTINCT a bulk collect INTO v_tl FROM test_num;
  v_tl.delete(2);--This remove 2nd element
  FORALL i IN INDICES OF v_tl
  INSERT INTO test_num_copy VALUES(v_tl(i));
END;
/
```

This will successfully copy the undeleted records into TABLE test_num_copy.

Advice 16.1: BULK COLLECT *OR* INITIALIZE a nested table

BULK COLLECT is used generally to populate a collection (PL/SQL table, nested table and Varray) in one go. Here we will discuss if we can process nested table/varray without initializing and extending.

Let us see the example:
```
CREATE OR REPLACE PACKAGE collection_pkg
IS
TYPE plsql_tab IS TABLE OF NUMBER INDEX BY PLS_INTEGER;
TYPE nest_tab IS  TABLE OF  NUMBER;
TYPE varr IS VARRAY (10) OF NUMBER;
END collection_pkg;
/
```

If you use "nested table collection **nest_tab** or varray collection **varr**" it will fail with error.
```
SET serveroutput ON
DECLARE
  v_collection collection_pkg.nest_tab;
BEGIN
  v_collection(1) :=100;
  dbms_output.put_line( 'First val is = '||v_collection (v_collection.FIRST));
END;
/
```
This will error out:
```
ORA-06531: Reference to uninitialized collection
```

To resolve this we have 2 solutions

Approach 1: INITIALIZE & EXTEND nested table

Initialize the nested table and extend the nested table as highlighted below:

```
SET serveroutput ON
DECLARE
  v_collection collection_pkg.nest_tab :=collection_pkg.nest_tab();
BEGIN
  v_collection.extend;
  v_collection(1) :=100;
  dbms_output.put_line( 'First val is = '||v_collection (v_collection.FIRST));
END;
/
```

Approach 2: Use BULK COLLECT

Use bulk collect, which eliminates the need of initialization as well as the need to extend a collection.

```
SET serveroutput ON
DECLARE
  v_collection collection_pkg.nest_tab ;
BEGIN
  SELECT 100 bulk collect INTO v_collection FROM dual;
  dbms_output.put_line( 'First val is = '||v_collection (v_collection.FIRST));
END;
/
```

Advice 17: PIPELINE function *OR* NON-PIPELINED function

Pipelining table function works similar to FIRST_ROW hint i.e. it does not wait for entire result-set to be constructed before returning the result. It returns the result of the pipelining table function using PIPE ROW command.

Non-pipelined function (normal function) works similar to ALL_ROWS hint i.e. it waits for entire result-set to be constructed before returning the result.

Approach 1: non-pipeline function

```
CREATE OR REPLACE type n_typ IS TABLE OF NUMBER;
CREATE OR REPLACE FUNCTION non_pipe_fl(a NUMBER) RETURN n_typ
IS
    l_row n_typ :=n_typ();
BEGIN
    l_row.extend;
    FOR I IN 1..a LOOP
    l_row(i) :=i;
    l_row.extend;
    END LOOP;
    RETURN l_row;
END non_pipe_fl;
/
```

Now when you run the below query:

```
SELECT * FROM TABLE(non_pipe_fl(900000)) WHERE rownum<10;
```

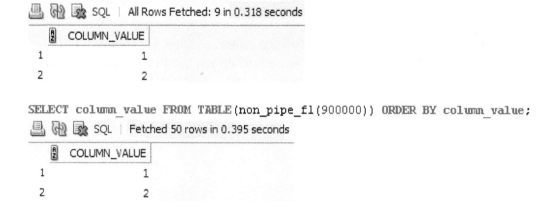

SELECT column_value FROM TABLE(non_pipe_fl(900000)) ORDER BY column_value;

SQL | Fetched 50 rows in 0.395 seconds

	COLUMN_VALUE
1	1
2	2

Approach 2: pipelined function

```
CREATE OR REPLACE type n_typ IS TABLE OF NUMBER;

CREATE OR REPLACE FUNCTION pipe_fl(a NUMBER) RETURN n_typ PIPELINED
IS
BEGIN
   FOR I IN 1..a LOOP
    PIPE ROW(i);
   END LOOP;
   RETURN;
END pipe_fl;
/
```

Now when you run the below query:

SELECT * FROM TABLE(pipe_fl(900000)) WHERE rownum<10;

SQL | All Rows Fetched: 9 in 0.001 seconds

	COLUMN_VALUE
1	1
2	2

SELECT column_value FROM TABLE(pipe_fl(900000)) ORDER BY column_value;

SQL | Fetched 50 rows in 0.191 seconds

	COLUMN_VALUE
1	1
2	2

You can observe that pipelined function works significantly faster than non-pipelined function for 1st few rows. However for all rows both works almost equally.

33

NOCOPY is compiler hint which passes IN OUT parameter by means of reference instead of value. For normal IN OUT parameter, actual and formal parameter refer to different memory location whereas when you use IN OUT NOCOPY then actual and formal parameter refer to same memory location.

Approach 1: passing parameter as IN OUT

Let us take one example:

```
CREATE OR REPLACE type n_typ IS TABLE OF NUMBER;
/

CREATE OR REPLACE PROCEDURE in_out_proc(l_tab IN OUT n_typ)
IS
BEGIN
 NULL;
END in_out_proc;
/
```

Now pass 10000000 values to the IN OUT procedure

```
SET SERVEROUTPUT ON
DECLARE
  v_tl n_typ :=n_typ();
  v_start number;
  v_end number;
BEGIN
   v_tl.extend;
   v_tl.extend(10000000,1);
   v_start :=DBMS_UTILITY.GET_TIME;
   in_out_proc(v_tl);
   v_end :=DBMS_UTILITY.GET_TIME;
DBMS_OUTPUT.PUT_LINE('Total time taken for IN OUT:'||(v_end-v_start));
END;
/
```

The output:
```
anonymous block completed
Total time taken for IN OUT:48
```

Approach 2: passing parameter as IN OUT NOCOPY

Let us take one example:

```
CREATE OR REPLACE type n_typ IS TABLE OF NUMBER;
/


CREATE OR REPLACE PROCEDURE in_out_nocopy_proc(l_tab IN OUT NOCOPY n_typ)
IS
BEGIN
 NULL;
END in_out_nocopy_proc;
/
```

Now pass 10000000 values to the IN OUT NOCOPY procedure

```
SET SERVEROUTPUT ON
DECLARE
   v_tl n_typ :=n_typ();
   v_start number;
   v_end number;
BEGIN
    v_tl.extend;
    v_tl.extend(10000000,1);
    v_start :=DBMS_UTILITY.GET_TIME;
    in_out_nocopy_proc(v_tl);
    v_end :=DBMS_UTILITY.GET_TIME;
DBMS_OUTPUT.PUT_LINE('Total time taken for nocopy:'||(v_end-v_start));
END;
/
```

The output:
```
anonymous block completed
Total time taken for nocopy:0
```

IN OUT NOCOPY performs faster because it does not copy actual parameter into formal parameter, instead it refers to the memory location of the actual parameter.

Advice 19: Package state throughout session *OR* duration of execution

Package cursor and **package variable** state persisted throughout the session is the default behaviour. Using **pragma serially_reusable** we can change the behaviour so that the cursor and variable state is persisted only for the duration of the **call/execution** (Not throughout the session).

Option 1: Package state for duration of execution/call

When you are short of PGA memory and your program refer to cursor which holds large amount of data and may potentially cause PGA swapping issue in those scenario we intend to use the state of the package state only for the duration of execution.
That means once the execution is over the package state is discarded and in next subsequent call package is again re-instated.
The advantage of this approach is that you do not hold the variable/cursor in the PGA memory for a long time. As soon as the execution is over PGA flush out the cursor/variable related with the package.

35

This is implemented using PRAGMA SERIALLY_REUSABLE

Take one example:

```
CREATE OR REPLACE PACKAGE time_pkg
IS
  PRAGMA SERIALLY_REUSABLE;
  X VARCHAR2(30) :=TO_CHAR(sysdate,'dd-mm-yyyy hh24:mi:ss');
END time_pkg;
/


  SET serveroutput ON
  BEGIN
    dbms_output.put_line(time_pkg.X);
  END;
  /
```

This return exact time in seconds when it is executed each time as below.

Anonymous block completed
26-04-2016 18:05:06

Anonymous block completed
26-04-2016 18:05:07

Using this PRAGMA, a cursor declared in package specification need not be closed as it is open only for the duration of the execution.
Using PRAGMA serially_reusable can reduce the load on PGA by not storing any value throughout the session. This feature is in contrast of package initialization which load the package in memory and persists across the session.

Option 2: Package state for throughout session

If you just comment out the line PRAGMA SERIALLY_REUSABLE then the above output will always be same.
Anonymous block completed
26-04-2016 18:05:06

Anonymous block completed
26-04-2016 18:05:06

Anonymous block completed
26-04-2016 18:05:06

Anonymous block completed
26-04-2016 18:05:06

As long as the session persist, all the cursor/variable will be present in the PGA because by default the package variable value persists throughout the session.

Both option 1 and option 2 has positive and negative side.

36

When you are not worried about memory and your sole concern is to improve performance of package call, then go for option 2.

When you are short of PGA memory which result in excessive swapping and degrade performance go for option 1.

Advice 20: Identify performance issue during compilation *OR* execution

Here we will discuss how to identify potential performance issues and presence of unwanted code during compilation instead of runtime.

Option 1: Identify issues at compile time

From oracle 10g onward we can identify potential performance issues and presence of unnecessary code through warning messages during compilation and accordingly modify or repair your code to make it more robust in terms of performance and scalability.

Example 1 performance issue:

```
ALTER SESSION SET PLSQL_WARNINGS='ENABLE:ALL';

CREATE TABLE SORTING_TEST
  (
    SYS_ID        VARCHAR2(30) PRIMARY KEY,
    APARTMENT_NO VARCHAR2(20)
  );

INSERT INTO SORTING_TEST VALUES(1123,'XX/YY');
INSERT INTO SORTING_TEST VALUES(1124,'XX/rY');
INSERT INTO SORTING_TEST VALUES(1125,'XX/pY');
INSERT INTO SORTING_TEST VALUES(1126,'XX/mY');
INSERT INTO SORTING_TEST VALUES(1127,'XX/nY');

COMMIT;

CREATE OR REPLACE PROCEDURE WARN_PROC
IS
 var_id number :=1125;
 v_apt_no varchar2(30);
BEGIN
 SELECT APARTMENT_NO INTO v_apt_no FROM SORTING_TEST where SYS_ID=var_id;
END WARN_PROC;
/
```

This procedure will give the following warning during compilation

⚠ Warning(6,60): PLW-07204: conversion away from column type may result in sub-optimal query plan

Because in table "**SORTING_TEST**" the column SYS_ID is of data type VARCHAR2 however the variable "var_id" used in the procedure is number and hence it will force internal data type conversion from number to char which results in bad performance.

Example 2 unnecessary code identification:

```
CREATE OR REPLACE PROCEDURE proc_warning
IS
  x NUMBER :=12;
  PROCEDURE junk_code
  IS
  BEGIN
    NULL;
  END junk_code;
BEGIN
  DBMS_OUTPUT.put_line ('value of x is:'||x);
END proc_warning;
/
```

This procedure will give the following warning during compilation

⚠ Warning(1,1): PLW-05018: unit PROC_WARNING omitted optional AUTHID clause; default value DEFINER used

⚠ Warning(6,4): PLW-06006: uncalled procedure "JUNK_CODE" is removed.

Because in the procedure <u>we have **not**</u> used "AUTHID DEFINER" and "JUNK_CODE" is <u>unnecessary</u> and hence needs to be removed otherwise this will add to the maintenance cost.

Note the procedure does not contain any error and hence when you fire

```
SHOW ERRORS PROCEDURE proc_warning
```

It will return no error and hence you can use your code as it is.

To check whether the warning flag is set in your database, use the following command:

```
SET serveroutput ON
BEGIN
  dbms_output.put_line('PLSQL warning is:'||$$PLSQL_WARNINGS);
END;
/
```

This will output:

```
PLSQL warning is:ENABLE:ALL
```

Option 2: Identify issues at run/execution time

If the WARNING is not set then at compile time issue will not be identified.
If the issue is not identified at compile time you may encounter degradation in performance and then while analysing explain plan you will observe that there is implicit conversion which led to the index being avoided. And then you rectify your code.

This is how we can find the issue at run time.
Either we set trace on and get tkprof output or individually analyzing the query.

For this case the query is (taken from the procedure created in OPTION 1):

```
SELECT APARTMENT_NO INTO v_apt_no FROM SORTING_TEST where SYS_ID=var_id;
```
And var_id=1125

So if we run explain plan:
```
SELECT APARTMENT_NO FROM SORTING_TEST where SYS_ID=1125;
```

38

OPERATION	OBJECT_NAME	COST	LAST_CR_BUFFER_GETS
⊟ ● SELECT STATEMENT		3	
⊟ ▦ TABLE ACCESS (FULL)	SORTING_TEST	3	8
⊟ ◯ Filter Predicates			
└── TO_NUMBER(SYS_ID)=1125			

You can clearly see sys_id is internally converted into TO_NUMBER (SYS_ID) which resulted in ignoring the primary key/index and hence full table scan.

The solution is to modify the procedure to use correct data type.

So enabling warning is powerful way to tune your code before it is executed.

Advice 21: Release-dependent code *OR* Release-independent code

Release-dependent code:
This is Default behaviour. This means code is related with specific release version of Oracle. In other words if you are in release 11g of Oracle then you can only use code/feature specific to Oracle 11g or below.

Oracle release-independent code means even if you are in release 11g of Oracle still you can keep code related with Oracle 11g, oracle 10g, oracle 12c.

Oracle release independent code is implemented using conditional compilation.

"**CONDITIONAL COMPILATION**" is introduced in Oracle 10gR2. This process excludes or includes <u>certain portions of code</u> at the time of compilation.

This means an API can contain both OLD and NEW versions of code, in other words this lets you create version independent code. Pre-12c environment you can compile the code which contains 12c related new features. This is possible because $IF/$ELSE are pre-processor **selection directives** which will selectively exclude certain portions of code during compilation.
E.g.

```
ALTER session SET PLSQL_CCFLAGS='version_12c: true';

CREATE OR REPLACE
PROCEDURE version_independent_p
IS
BEGIN
  $IF $$version_12c $then
  --Use code related WITH 12c NEW feature LIKE match_recognize clause;
$ELSE
--Use code prior TO 12c feature;
$END
END;
/
```

This will compile fine in 11g also even though **match_recognize** clause <u>is undefined in</u> Oracle 11g as it was introduced in 12c (in 11g you must set **version_12c :false**).

"Version_12c" is a <u>user defined</u> <u>**inquiry directive**</u>. This is set using **PLSQL_CCFLAGS initialization parameter** (This parameter allow PL/SQL programmer to control conditional compilation of each PL/SQL unit).
We have <u>predefined</u> **inquiry directives** like PLSQL_LINE, PLSQL_UNIT, PLSQL_DEBUG, PLSQL_WARNINGS etc. All the inquiry directives **are prefixed by $$** as shown in the example above.

Advice 22: Function Based Index *OR* Indexed Virtual column in 11g?

Here we will discuss how to create Index on a function/expression. Also we will explore how to create index on a column which is derived and virtual in nature.

Next we will have comparative analysis between **<u>FBI (Function Based Index)</u>** and **<u>Indexed Virtual column</u>**.

Function based index was introduced in Oracle 8i, it is an index which is created on the function of a table column. So instead of indexing a column we are indexing the result of a function on the column.
The function can be an oracle function or a user defined function.

Note that to create a <u>function based index</u> on a user defined function you need to make sure the *user define function* is deterministic, otherwise <u>function based index</u> will not work.

You can query DBA_IND_EXPRESSIONS table to see the details of the expression in a function based index. Note the indexed expression (like UPPER (name)) is stored as hidden virtual column for the table being indexed.

Oracle Virtual Column was introduced in Oracle 11g, it is a derived/pre-computed value using either oracle function or user defined function or an expression.

Note that to create a <u>virtual column</u> in a table based on a user defined function, you need to make sure the *user define function* is deterministic, otherwise <u>virtual column</u> creation will not work using that function.

Let us take a simple example

This function will find the occurrence of a string in the main string:

```
CREATE OR REPLACE
  FUNCTION f_Count_occurrences(
     p_string    IN CLOB,
     p_substring IN VARCHAR2)
   RETURN NUMBER
   deterministic ←─────────────────────     This clause is mandatory here
                                             For the function to be indexed
   IS
     l_occurrences NUMBER;
   BEGIN
    IF ( p_string   IS NOT NULL AND p_substring IS NOT NULL ) THEN
      l_occurrences := ( LENGTH(p_string) - ( NVL(LENGTH(REPLACE(p_string, p_substring)), 0) ) ) / LENGTH(p_substring) ;
    END IF;
    RETURN ( l_occurrences );
  END f_count_occurrences;

drop table test11;
Create table test11(class_processed varchar2(34));
insert into test11 values('123/456');
insert into test11 values('123/456/44');
insert into test11 values('123/456/2/3/4/5');
insert into test11 values('123/456/6/7/78/899#88#56');
```

Function used for <u>function based index</u>:

```
create index test11_f_Count_occurrences_idx on test11(f_Count_occurrences(class_processed,'/'));

select f_Count_occurrences(class_processed,'/') from  test11;
select f_Count_occurrences(class_processed,'#') from  test11;
```

Function used for <u>oracle virtual column</u>:

```
alter table test11 add(class_proc_count2 generated always as (f_Count_occurrences(class_processed,'#')) virtual);
```

Alternatively, to create a table with a virtual column and "index on that virtual column":

Virtual column

```
Create table test112(class_processed varchar2(34),class_proc_cnt as (f_Count_occurrences(class_processed,'/')));
insert into test112(class_processed) values('123/456');
insert into test112(class_processed) values('123/456/44');
insert into test112(class_processed) values('123/456/2/3/4/5');
insert into test112(class_processed) values('123/456/6/7/78/899#88#56');
commit;
create index test112_cnt_idx on test112(class_proc_cnt);
select * from test112;
```

User defined Function

Some observations:

1. You cannot create a <u>function based index</u> and <u>virtual column</u> on the same expression, so for understanding we cannot create both for expression

    ```
    f_Count_occurrences(class_processed,'/')
    ```

2. When you use virtual column based on normal computation like commission as **salary/100** or **salary*10/bonus** then virtual column usage is better than function based index because we have to create the function and need to index it against the column.

3. When you use virtual column you need to maintain the DDL required to create the virtual column but function based index can be independently added/altered/dropped.

4. Virtual column can refer to column from the same table where it is defined.

Virtual column can be indexed like a normal column. We have seen many cases the performance gain by using **indexed virtual column** is more than using function based index. However often both perform equally. So you need to test both the concepts for your scenario before deciding which one performs better for your scenarios.

Advice 23: Invisible index *OR* drop & recreate Index *OR* Virtual Index

To test efficacy of certain index you need to make an index unusable for certain duration.
There are **3 ways** to implement this.

```
CREATE TABLE empl AS SELECT * FROM emp;

CREATE INDEX empl_id_idx ON empl
  (employee_id
  );
```

Option 1: Drop/recreate Index

```
DROP INDEX empl_id_idx;
```
Test your application without the index
```
CREATE INDEX empl_id_idx ON empl
  (employee_id
  );
```

Alternatively you can make the index unusable for the observation period

```
ALTER INDEX empl_id_idx UNUSABLE;
```
Test your application without the index
```
ALTER INDEX empl_id_idx REBUILD;
```

Both Drop/Create and UNUSABLE/REBUILD operations are very costly for large tables.

Option 2: Make the index Invisible and then visible

Invisible index was introduced in Oracle 11gR1.
The solution is to make the index invisible for the duration of testing and then make it visible.

```
ALTER INDEX empl_id_idx INVISIBLE;
```

Test your application
```
ALTER INDEX empl_id_idx VISIBLE;
```

Making the index visible/invisible is very fast and incur almost no cost.

Invisible index is an index which is maintained by the database, however it is ignored by the optimizer with its default setting.
If the **OPTIMIZER_USE_INVISIBLE_INDEXES** parameter is set to **FALSE** (which is the default setting) then the invisible index is not used unless you use oracle hint.

To create an invisible index the syntax is
```
CREATE INDEX index_inv ON table_name  (column_name) INVISIBLE;
```
You can view if an index is visible or invisible using:
```
SELECT index_name, visibility FROM dba_indexes WHERE index_name='INDEX_INV';
```

In order to use the Invisible index you need to do <u>one of the following</u> activities

➤ Setting using parameter:
```
ALTER SESSION SET OPTIMIZER_USE_INVISIBLE_INDEXES=TRUE; --Session level

ALTER SYSTEM SET OPTIMIZER_USE_INVISIBLE_INDEXES =TRUE; --System level
```


➤ Use hint **USE_INVISIBLE_INDEXES** in select statement from 11gR2 onward

```
SELECT /*+ USE_INVISIBLE_INDEXES */
  ...from table_name;
```

If you use the <u>index hint</u> as below in 11gR1 (only), invisible index will be used.
```
SELECT /*+ INDEX(table_name index_inv) */
  ...FROM table_name;
```
However the above <u>index hints</u> will be ignored for invisible index from 11gR2 onward and hence you have to use hint **USE_INVISIBLE_INDEXES** if you want to use the invisible index.

➤ Invisible index if present will be automatically invoked and help resolve table lock on parent table for missing index on foreign key column.

<u>Invisible index</u> is used in the following situations:

➤ There are situations where we need to test if a particular index is impacting an application positively or negatively. Before 11g we need to drop the index or make the index unusable to test that. After the test we need to make it usable and rebuild the index which is a very costly operation.

However in 11g you can do that by using invisible index. Once it is invisible you can check how your query performs without the index and accordingly you can decide if you can either drop the index or make it visible for regular usage by all the applications and thus avoid a costly rebuild operation.
We just make an index visible/invisible using simple command

```
ALTER INDEX index_name INVISIBLE;
```
And after the test we can make it visible
```
ALTER INDEX index_name VISIBLE;
```

Later we can drop the index if the index is not required

➢ The <u>invisible index</u> is used when a certain module in an application requires a specific index whereas another module of the application must not use that index. So using hints as shown above we are able to selectively use the index without impacting the whole application in terms of response time (only select operation). However you must check the impact **on the throughput** of the application as Oracle <u>will continue to store</u> all the details in terms of cardinality, uniqueness, space usage and all other metadata related attributes

➢ <u>Invisible index</u> is used to associate primary key with unique index to non-unique index and vice versa as shown in subsequent advice in the book

Option 3: Virtual Index (NOSEGMENT)

As the name suggested virtual index will let you test an index if it really existed in the database without creating a real index.

Virtual indexes is an object which helps us simulate the existence of an index - without actually building a full index. So if you have a very large index that you want to create without allocating space and to determine if the index would be used by the optimizer then create one virtual index.

This virtual index is nothing but an index created with NOSEGMENT. This allows you to test and tune your application. Sometime this virtual index is called "**fake index**" because they do not really exists. When you are using the virtual index it will tell in the **execution plan** if the index will be used potentially however in **execution time** oracle may prefer not to use the index. The "virtual index" is meant for only checking if the index could be useful <u>if it really existed</u> in the database.

First, note that virtual indexes are only enabled for a session that sets a certain parameter as below:
```
ALTER Session SET "_use_nosegment_indexes" = TRUE;
```

Now, create the virtual index, using the special keyword **NOSEGMENT**:

```
CREATE INDEX Index_V ON TABLE_NAME  (Column_name)
NOSEGMENT compute statistics;
```

With the index in place, simply use explain plan as usual to see if the index is used as below:
```
Explain plan FOR SELECT * FROM (TABLE_NAME);
SELECT plan_table_output
FROM TABLE(dbms_xplan.display('plan_table',NULL,'serial'));
```

To find if there is any virtual index present in the database just run:
```
SELECT index_owner,
   index_name
FROM dba_ind_columns
WHERE index_name NOT LIKE 'BIN$%'
MINUS
SELECT owner, index_name FROM dba_indexes;
```

44

This is quite intriguing as to how to reduce database downtime and avoid subsequent issues (whilst a new type of index is created after old index is dropped). There are 2 ways to deal with this.

Approach 1: Drop and create index

This is conventional approach where we need to drop the index and then create new type of index. This process may take certain amount of time and for that period your application is susceptible to data integrity and poor response time because index is not available for some amount of time.
Note: you cannot reduce downtime at all in this approach

Approach 2: Create multiple index on that column

In this approach we can reduce the downtime by maintaining different kinds of indexes on the same column. By doing this you can guarantee that index is always present and hence resolve data integrity and poor response time as experienced in approach 1. Also you reduce downtime to zero.

Having **multiple indexes** on same set of columns allows you to switch between indexes based on situation and application requirement and also lets you quickly see the impact of various types of index on the same set of columns in the application. Multiple indexes will be useful when you want to convert from one type of index to other type of index with a minimal downtime. However only one of the indexes on the column will be visible at single point of time.

Also note we can create more than 1 index on 1 column or set of columns only if index type **is different and one of the index is visible at single point of time**.

Pre **12c** we could never create more than 1 index on 1 column or set of columns. In **12c only** we can do that.

Note in Oracle 11gR1 **invisible index** was introduced as shown in previous tips. Now we have to use the invisible index concept to create multiple indexes on same column.
E.g.

```
CREATE TABLE EMP(EMPNO NUMBER,ENAME VARCHAR2(30),SAL NUMBER,HIRE_DATE DATE);
INSERT INTO EMP VALUES(1,'STEVE',2546,SYSDATE-100);
INSERT INTO EMP VALUES(2,'JOHN',2547,SYSDATE-140);
INSERT INTO EMP VALUES(1,'ALEEN',2548,SYSDATE-160);
COMMIT;


CREATE INDEX emp_idx_1 ON EMP
  (empno,ename
  );


CREATE Bitmap INDEX emp_idx_2 ON EMP
  (
    empno,ename
  )
INVISIBLE;
```

Note one of the indexes is invisible and both indexes are of different type. You can change this anytime as below:

```
ALTER INDEX emp_idx_1 INVISIBLE;
ALTER INDEX emp_idx_2 VISIBLE;
```

You can even create **unique** and **non-unique** index on the same set of columns.

```
CREATE UNIQUE INDEX E_U_IDX ON EMP(ENAME);
ALTER INDEX E_U_IDX INVISIBLE;
CREATE INDEX E_NU_IDX ON EMP(ENAME);
```

Advice 25: Index on foreign key column *OR* no index on foreign key column

Here we will discuss both the approach and pitfalls.

Approach 1: Index on Foreign Key Column

Having **foreign key index** provides the following benefits:

When parent and child tables are joined on the foreign key column then the foreign key index will **result into nested loop join** and this in turn improve response time and thus improve performance of your application.

For the duration of child table modification the parent table is not locked.

However as a rule of thumb do not create index on all foreign key columns. Check your application requirement and workflow and take a call if it is required to create the index on foreign key column. Too many index impact throughput of an application.

Approach 2: No Index on Foreign Key Column

Without index on foreign key column, parent table get locked for the duration of child table modification which degrade performance in terms of response time and throughput.

Oracle places an <u>exclusive lock</u> on a child table if you do not index the foreign key constraint in that child table and you are trying to modify the corresponding child and parent table.
This will show in **v$session** wait event: **"enq: TM – contention"** this indicates there are un-indexed foreign key constraints.

Take the **example** below

```
CREATE TABLE emp  (empid NUMBER PRIMARY KEY, deptid NUMBER  );
CREATE TABLE dept  (deptid NUMBER PRIMARY KEY  );
ALTER TABLE emp ADD CONSTRAINT emp_fk FOREIGN KEY(  deptid) REFERENCES dept
(deptid);

INSERT INTO dept VALUES (10 );
INSERT INTO dept VALUES (20 );
INSERT INTO emp VALUES (1,10 );
INSERT INTO emp VALUES (2,20 );
COMMIT;
```

Now open 2 Oracle sql **sessions:**

Session 1

Modify any record from child table EMP.
e.g.
```
DELETE FROM emp WHERE deptid = 10;
```

Do not commit

Session 2
Try to modify any record of parent table DEPT, it will simply hang
e.g.
```
DELETE FROM dept WHERE deptid = 20;
```

Please note Oracle will place an exclusive lock on the whole table even if you are modifying a single record and the **record is different** from the one you are updating in **Session 1**

You can see from v$session, the TM lock by running the query:
```
SELECT l.sid,
    s.blocking_session blocker_session,
    s.event,
    l.type,
    l.lmode,
    l.request,
    o.object_name,
    o.object_type
FROM v$lock l,
    dba_objects o,
    v$session s
WHERE UPPER (s.username) = UPPER ('U1')
AND l.id1              = o.object_id (+)
AND l.sid             = s.sid;
```

The output look as below:

SID	BLOCKER_SESSION	EVENT	TYPE	LMODE	REQUEST	OBJECT_NAME	OBJECT_TYPE
10	(null)	SQL*Net message from client	AE	4	0	ORA$BASE	EDITION
10	(null)	SQL*Net message from client	TM	3	0	EMP	TABLE
10	(null)	SQL*Net message from client	TM	2	0	DEPT	TABLE
10	(null)	SQL*Net message from client	TX	6	0	(null)	(null)
247	10	enq: TM - contention	AE	4	0	ORA$BASE	EDITION
247	10	enq: TM - contention	TM	0	4	EMP	TABLE

To resolve the lock you must have an index on the foreign key column of the child table as below
```
CREATE INDEX emp_fk ON emp
  (deptid
  );
```
Note: Even if you create invisible index (instead of default visible index), still it will resolve the table lock issue.
       Also you must make sure there is no child record present when you will attempt to delete from parent table.

The following query identifies which tables are affected because of not having an index on the foreign key column of the child table

47

```
SELECT *
FROM
    (SELECT a.constraint_name cons_name ,
        a.table_name tab_name ,
        b.column_name cons_column ,
        NVL(c.column_name,'***No foreign key Index***') ind_column
    FROM dba_constraints a
    JOIN all_cons_columns b
    ON a.constraint_name = b.constraint_name
    LEFT OUTER JOIN all_ind_columns c
    ON b.column_name      = c.column_name
    AND b.table_name      = c.table_name
    WHERE a.owner         ='SCHEMA_NAME'
    AND a.constraint_type = 'R'
    )
WHERE ind_column='***No foreign key Index***';
```

This will list out all the foreign key columns which do not have an associated index for that foreign key column in the child table.

Another **disadvantage of missing foreign key index** is as below:
When parent and child tables are joined on the foreign key column then the absence of foreign key index will **result into sort merge join** or **full table scan instead of nested loop join** and this in turn increase the response time and degrade performance of your application.

Advice 26: Index skip scan *OR* Index range scan

Here we will discuss both the approach and see how by converting index skip scan to index range scan result in dropping execution time from 4 hr. to 10 seconds.

Approach 1: Index skip scan

Index skip scan let a concatenated index be used in a query even if leading edge predicate is skipped in multi-column index.
We have table "XXX" with millions of records. In this table columns "exact_date","pnr" and "svcno" has a <u>unique index</u>.

Also this table has concatenated <u>non unique index</u> "idx_mon_date" on the set of columns [month_date (This store only mmyyyy), Tno, amt]

Now we have the requirement to get the report for a period **1/4/2012** to **15/4/2012**
This is the query:

```
SELECT pnr,
  Drum,
  Tno,
  amt
FROM xxx
WHERE Tno IN ('3234', '5678', '9786', '4567')
AND exact_date BETWEEN '20120401' AND '20120415'
AND amt  = '0'
AND Drum = '0';
```

This query takes more than 4 hours to execute, when the period is increased so too does the execution time.
Table is analyzed and data is structured properly. All indexes are in proper place and rebuilt and analyzed. There is no **distinct cause** for the **slowness** of the query. But it is a very critical report and needs to be published soon.

The **explain plan** for the query is as below:

```
--------------------------------------------------------------------------------------------------------
| Id | Operation                         | Name        | Rows  | Bytes | Cost (%CPU)| Time     | Pstart| Pstop |
--------------------------------------------------------------------------------------------------------
|  0 | SELECT STATEMENT                  |             |     1 |    41 |  376K  (1)| 01:27:57 |       |       |
|  1 |  PARTITION RANGE ALL              |             |     1 |    41 |  376K  (1)| 01:27:57 |     1 |  3422 |
|* 2 |   TABLE ACCESS BY LOCAL INDEX ROWID| xxx        |     1 |    41 |  376K  (1)| 01:27:57 |     1 |  3422 |
|* 3 |    INDEX SKIP SCAN                | idx_mon_date| 6629K |       | 30471  (1)| 00:07:07 |     1 |  3422 |
--------------------------------------------------------------------------------------------------------
```

Approach 2: Index range scan

Index range scan is a scan on a non-unique index which will return set of rows.

We will discuss tactical solution to convert index skip scan to index range scan.

A close look onto the explain plan of approach 1, shows **distinctly** there is an **index skip scan** on "idx_mon_date". Actually the **index skip scan** was introduced to allow Oracle to "skip" leading-edge predicates in a multi-column index so that our concatenated index can be used in the query.

Oracle state that the **index skip scan** is not as fast as **a direct index lookup**, but states that the **index skip scan** is faster than a **full-table scan**. So large tables with concatenated indexes, the index skip-scan feature can provide quick access even when the leading column of the index is not used in a limiting condition and hence give better performance as against full table scan.

However for this case if we introduce "**month_date**" column in the query "where" clause we get **INDEX RANGE SCAN** as the predicate (leading edge column is present for index idx_mon_date)

```
SELECT pnr,
  Drum,
  Tno,
  amt
FROM xxx
WHERE Tno IN ('3234', '5678', '9786', '4567')
AND exact_date BETWEEN '20120401' AND '20120415'
AND month_date='042012'
AND amt       = '0'
AND Drum      = '0';
```

And here is the execution plan

```
| Id | Operation                            | Name        | Rows  | Bytes | Cost (%CPU) | Time     | Pstart | Pstop |
|----|--------------------------------------|-------------|-------|-------|-------------|----------|--------|-------|
|  0 | SELECT STATEMENT                     |             |     1 |    48 | 10130   (1) | 00:02:22 |        |       |
|  1 |  PARTITION RANGE ALL                 |             |     1 |    48 | 10130   (1) | 00:02:22 |      1 |  3422 |
|* 2 |   TABLE ACCESS BY LOCAL INDEX ROWID  | XXX         |     1 |    48 | 10130   (1) | 00:02:22 |      1 |  3422 |
|* 3 |    INDEX RANGE SCAN                  | idx_mon_date| 62185 |  6881 |     (1)     | 00:01:37 |      1 |  3422 |
```

The execution time drop to **10 seconds** (it was taking **more than 4 hrs.** before the change)

Advice 27: Use DATE column INDEX by function based index *OR* Refactor code

Let us say you have a table with column "**Exact_date DATE**". The **EXACT_DATE** column can store time portion (HH24:MI:SS) of the DATE. However as it stores the time portion (default behavior of DATE datatype) to get the result for a particulate DATE, you have to use TRUNC(EXACT_DATE) which in turn make the index not used.

We have 2 approaches for the solution:

Approach 1: Using Function based Index

Create function based index on TRUNC (Exact_date) and change the query filter criteria as below:
```
TRUNC(Exact_date)=to_date('20120401','YYYYMMDD')
```

Approach 2: Using Refactor Code

Instead of the below filter clause
```
Exact_date=to_date('20120401','YYYYMMDD')
```

Use the following filter criteria:
```
Exact_date>=  to_date('20120401','YYYYMMDD') AND
Exact_date<   to_date('20120401','YYYYMMDD')+1
```

This way you are able to use the index on "Exact_date" and you are able to cover all the 24 hrs. Period for the particular date.

Advice 28: Non Unique index with NULL values *OR* NOT NULL value for a column

Approach 1: Non Unique index with NULL values

A non-unique index may be created on any column that is widely used in an application.
As per the table definition the non-unique column can be nullable or not nullable.

If the column is defined as nullable and you query the table for the null value then there will be full table scan as Oracle does not index a null value.
You can create index on null values by creating function based index as discussed in this book.

Approach 2: Non Unique index with NOT NULL values

If you define the column as NOT NULL and when there is no value for the column then you can store a default value say "unknown", then when you query the table for the default value "unknown" Oracle will use the index and full table scan is eliminated

So as a general rule any column that always contain data should be declared as not null and there should be some default value, This will allow efficient index search instead of full table scan for null values.

Advice 29: Sorting table rows without using ORDER BY *OR* using ORDER BY

Sorting is the process by which all the data returned by a query is arranged in certain order for you to analyse the data effectively. Sorting is a very costly operation and requires a lot of work to be done by the Oracle engine.

There are 2 ways we can do sorting

Sorting using ORDER BY clause:

In oracle using "ORDER BY column-name ASC" and "ORDER BY column-name DESC" allows you to sort the result-set in ascending or descending order respectively.

Since sorting is very costly operation its avoidance is one of the challenges for the **dba/developer**.

Sorting without using ORDER BY clause:

Here are the steps to order the data without using ORDER BY clause and avoid the costly sorting operation.

Approach 1: Create an index on the ordering columns. In this case even if you use order by in your query it does not use sorting. Note the "ORDER BY" clause uses the index.

Approach 2: A common mistake an oracle developer makes is to specify the ORDER BY clause in a query even if the query is inherently sorted.
For example if you have a query with "WHERE" clause criteria and the "WHERE" clause column has index then the result-set will be returned as per the indexed column. So when you write a query which does not have any "WHERE" clause which needs to be sorted/ordered by certain column, in that case use a dummy "WHERE" clause like "empno>0" which will inherently use the index and sorting is avoided.

Approach 3: If you do not want to use a dummy where clause you can still order the data using hint as below:
Select /*+ INDEX_ASC (table_name specific index) */.....

If you want to sort the rows in descending order
Select /*+ INDEX_DESC (table_name specific index) */.....

Sample example to show how to avoid sorting:

```
CREATE TABLE batch_log
  (
    p_grp     VARCHAR2(30),
    batch_id NUMBER,
    unit_nm   VARCHAR2(30),
    tot_cnt   NUMBER
  );
ALTER TABLE batch_log ADD CONSTRAINT pk_batch_log PRIMARY KEY
(
  p_grp,batch_id,unit_nm
)
;
```

Now insert a set of records:
```
INSERT INTO batch_log VALUES
  ('grp1',1,'u1',100
  );
INSERT INTO batch_log VALUES
  ('grp1',3,'u1',200
  );
INSERT INTO batch_log VALUES
  ('grp1',2,'u1',300
  );
INSERT INTO batch_log VALUES
  ('grp1',4,'u1',400
  );
INSERT INTO batch_log VALUES
  ('grp2',4,'u1',500
  );
INSERT INTO batch_log VALUES
  ('grp1',6,'u1',600
  );
INSERT INTO batch_log VALUES
  ('grp1',5,'u1',400
  );
```

The result from the following query will be sorted by batch_id:
```
SELECT * FROM batch_log ORDER BY batch_id;
```

The explain plan shows that sorting is used:

OPERATION	OBJECT_NAME	OPTIONS
SELECT STATEMENT		
SORT		ORDER BY
TABLE ACCESS	BATCH_LOG	FULL

How can you avoid sorting? Even though batch_id column is part of the primary key "order by batch_id" uses sorting.

Solution 1
Create index on the batch_id column only. So if you create index on batch_id column only then even if you use order by clause in your query, it will not use sorting. Important to note the "ORDER BY" clause uses the index and hence sorting step is eliminated.
This is the solution using **approach 1** and you employ this approach in certain scenario, but for this case it is not advisable as you have a primary key on "p_grp, **batch_id**, unit_nm"

Solution 2

As explained in **approach 2**, if the "**where**" clause is on indexed columns then you do not need the "**order by**" clause as the data will be returned in index order. There is a huge gain in performance as a result of eliminating the expensive sorting.

```
SELECT *
FROM batch_log
WHERE p_grp='grp1'
AND batch_id BETWEEN 1 AND 10
AND unit_nm='u1';
```

The explain plan shows that sorting is not used but the result-set is inherently sorted:

OPERATION	OBJECT_NAME	OPTIONS
SELECT STATEMENT		
TABLE ACCESS	BATCH_LOG	BY INDEX ROWID
INDEX	PK_BATCH_LOG	RANGE SCAN
Access Predicates		
AND		
P_GRP='grp1'		
BATCH_ID>=1		
UNIT_NM='u1'		
BATCH_ID<=10		
Filter Predicates		
UNIT_NM='u1'		

Solution 3

As explained in **approach 3**, you can use the index hint

```
SELECT /*+ INDEX_ASC(batch_log pk_batch_log) */ * FROM batch_log;
```

The explain plan shows that sorting is not used but the result-set is inherently sorted:

OPERATION	OBJECT_NAME	OPTIONS
SELECT STATEMENT		
TABLE ACCESS	BATCH_LOG	BY INDEX ROWID
INDEX	PK_BATCH_LOG	FULL SCAN

Equipped with this understanding you can now re-write your query to use "where clause" instead of costly "order by clause" and so improve the performance of your query.

Advice 30: Primary key with UNIQUE index *OR* NON-UNIQUE index

Here we will discuss different ways to create association of unique and non-unique index to a primary key constraint in a table. We will have comparative analysis of both the approaches.

A **primary key** is a column in a table which uniquely identifies a row. In a sense Primary key is the same as a unique index but the differences are that
  ➢ **Primary key** cannot be null but unique index can be null.
  ➢ You can have one **primary key** in a table but any number of unique indexes in a table.
When a **primary key** is defined for a table oracle will automatically create an associated **unique index** for it.

However a **primary key** can be associated with a **unique index** or a **non-unique index** by decoupling primary key constraint and index as shown.

Approach 1: (Association with unique index):

Here is an example to show this:

```
CREATE TABLE test_constraint_t
  (
    a NUMBER,
    b VARCHAR2(30),
    c VARCHAR2(30),
    PRIMARY KEY(a)
  );
SELECT * FROM all_constraints WHERE table_name ='TEST_CONSTRAINT_T';
```

Output:

CONSTRAINT_NAME	CONSTRAINT_TYPE	TABLE_NAME
SYS_C00149342784	P	TEST_CONSTRAINT_T

```
SELECT * FROM all_indexes WHERE table_name ='TEST_CONSTRAINT_T';
```

Output:

INDEX_NAME	INDEX_TYPE	TABLE_OWNER	TABLE_NAME	TABLE_TYPE	UNIQUENESS
SYS_C00149346130	NORMAL	U1	TEST_CONSTRAINT_T	TABLE	UNIQUE

Approach 2: (Association with unique or non-unique index):

Here is an example to show how it is done.
```
CREATE TABLE test_constraint_t
  (
    a NUMBER,
    b VARCHAR2(30),
    c VARCHAR2(30)
  );
CREATE INDEX test_constraint_t_idx ON test_constraint_t(a);
ALTER TABLE test_constraint_t ADD CONSTRAINT TEST_CONSTRAINT_T_PK
PRIMARY KEY (a);
```
Note: Here you create a non-unique index for the primary key, however you can create unique index instead of non-unique index. So you can create just one index for the primary key or using approach 1 internally just one unique index is created. Adding the primary key constraint step as mentioned above won't create any additional unique index.

```
SELECT * FROM all_constraints WHERE table_name ='TEST_CONSTRAINT_T';
```
Output:

CONSTRAINT_NAME	CONSTRAINT_TYPE	TABLE_NAME
TEST_CONSTRAINT_T_PK	P	TEST_CONSTRAINT_T

```
SELECT * FROM all_indexes WHERE table_name ='TEST_CONSTRAINT_T';
```
Output:

INDEX_NAME	INDEX_TYPE	TABLE_OWNER	TABLE_NAME	TABLE_TYPE	UNIQUENESS
TEST_CONSTRAINT_T_IDX	NORMAL	U1	TEST_CONSTRAINT_T	TABLE	NONUNIQUE

Steps to associate primary key with different index(different columns from primary key) **test_constraint_t_idx1**:

54

```
CREATE INDEX test_constraint_t_idx1 ON test_constraint_t(a,b);
ALTER TABLE test_constraint_t MODIFY PRIMARY KEY USING INDEX test_constraint_t_idx1;
DROP INDEX test_constraint_t_idx;
```

Steps to associate primary key with unique index(same column as primary key) **test_constraint_t_idx2** from a non-unique index:

```
CREATE UNIQUE INDEX test_constraint_t_idx2 ON test_constraint_t(a) invisible;
ALTER TABLE test_constraint_t MODIFY PRIMARY KEY USING INDEX test_constraint_t_idx2;
ALTER INDEX test_constraint_t_idx2 VISIBLE;
DROP INDEX test_constraint_t_idx;
```

No matter whether you use <u>approach 1</u> or <u>approach 2</u> to associate the primary key with a unique or non-unique index, the primary key constraint always <u>maintains the uniqueness</u> of the column and returns just one record when you have index lookup.

When you <u>associate the primary key with unique or non-unique index</u> the behaviour is as below:
  ➤ Primary key associated with unique index then oracle use INDEX UNIQUE SCAN
  ➤ Primary key associated with non-unique index then oracle use INDEX RANGE SCAN
  ➤ Both the above cases the index lookup returns just 1 row.

It is preferable to use **approach 2** for the following reasons
  ➤ You can drop or disable the primary key constraint independent of the index
  ➤ You can make an index unusable independent of primary key constraint and then make it usable by rebuilding the index, in other words you can **decouple** constraint and index and hence independently disable either the constraint or the index. This flexibility helps to overcome severe performance degradation especially for batch loads which might consists of millions of transactions. By dropping the index (or making the index unusable) during batch load the throughput of batch load is improved considerably. After the batch load is completed the index is recreated and analyzed.
  ➤ You can associate the primary key with either UNIQUE or NON-UNIQUE index. But with **approach 1** you can associate only with UNIQUE index.
  ➤ You can give user defined name for primary key and indexes
  ➤ When large volume of data is present and you need to do certain operation which require disable/deferred/drop primary key you can do that using this **approach 2** and it <u>does not require to **rebuild the index**</u>.
  ➤ **Rebuilding index** is a process to reorganize an existing index. This operation consumes double the space of a single index because REBUILD index uses existing index as a source for reorganizing the index. Rebuild operation takes exclusive locks by default (offline mode)

Advice 31: Use index *OR* Avoid index

Index is a database object which is created in a table to find the data in that table more quickly without going through the whole table. However you should not create index in all scenarios.

Use Index:
  ➤ Columns that are used in WHERE clause, ORDER BY clause and GROUP BY clause
  ➤ It is recommended to create index on columns with high number of distinct values

Avoid Index:
  ➤ Columns that are very frequently undergoing changes require high maintenance and hence index on those columns should be avoided.

- Column that contains high number of NULL values causes data to be skewed towards NULL and hence index on those columns should be avoided.
- If a table is small and can be accessed with fewer I/O it is recommended not to use index on that table.
- If a column is used in "**WHERE**" clause but return high percentage of data, in that case it is recommended not to use index

Advice 32: Find Inter-rows pattern using Analytical function *OR* "MATCH_RECOGNISE" clause

With the advent of "BIG data" the requirement for creation and capture of more and more data is increasing day by day. Along with extra data, the business requirement of finding different patterns in data is growing rapidly.
A pattern is a repetitive series of events. Pattern can be found everywhere and in the current scenario of big data it is very much a business requirement to analyse a specific dataset and find a particular pattern.

Examples of real life scenarios can be
- Finding stock price ups and down pattern
- Finding malicious activity by some intruder
- Crime pattern
- Predict specific phone call pattern
- Fraud detection

Prior to 12c in order to detect a specific pattern it was a very difficult and complex job using analytic function, recursive queries using connect by and "WITH" clause and many self joins.
However in oracle 12c this pattern matching is simplified using "MATCH_RECOGNIZE" clause. This clause lets you take a dataset then group it into sets of data and order it based on timestamp and then look for a specific patterns in those partitions/groups.
Oracle Regular expression match pattern within the same record/row and 12c MATCH_RECOGNIZE match patterns across rows boundaries. So **regular expression** works for **intra-rows** whereas 12c **match_recognize** works for **inter-rows**.

Scenario1: Find all the animals which are registered consecutively as Red, blue, green and Yellow.

Scenario 1: Approach 1: Using Analytical function

Let us take one example of animal registration where each animal has a specific colour.
The requirement is to find the pattern where Red, Blue, Green and Yellow colour appear consecutively based on animal registration id.
Here you can see the specific colour combination appears 2 times.

2	G
3	G
4	B
5	G
6	R
7	B
8	G
9	Y
10	R
11	B
12	Y
13	G
14	R
15	B
16	G
17	Y
18	G

Pattern for consecutive colours R,B,G,Y

Pattern for consecutive colours R,B,G,Y

In order to get the pattern prior to 12 you need to write the following analytic query which will give the animal_ids for which the pattern is found.

Prior to 12c Solution:

```
create table anilmal_colour(animal_id number,colour varchar2(10));
insert into anilmal_colour values(1,'Red');
insert into anilmal_colour values(2,'Yellow');
insert into anilmal_colour values(3,'Green');
insert into anilmal_colour values(4,'Red');
insert into anilmal_colour values(5,'Green');
insert into anilmal_colour values(6,'Yellow');
insert into anilmal_colour values(7,'Red');
insert into anilmal_colour values(8,'Red');
insert into anilmal_colour values(9,'Red');
insert into anilmal_colour values(10,'Red');
insert into anilmal_colour values(11,'Blue');
insert into anilmal_colour values(12,'Green');
insert into anilmal_colour values(13,'Yellow');
commit;
```

The analytic query to get the pattern:

```
                    SELECT *
                    FROM anilmal_colour
                    WHERE (animal_id) IN
                       (SELECT regexp_substr(animal_ids_str,'[^,]+',1,level)  ←─────────
                        FROM                                                    This will display all the ids in unpivoted rows
                           (SELECT animal_id
                            ||','
                            ||next_animal_id
                            ||','
                            ||second_next_animal_id
                            ||','
                            ||third_next_animal_id animal_ids_str
                         FROM
                           (SELECT d.*,
                          ─→lead(colour) over(order by animal_id) next_colour,
                            lead(animal_id) over(order by animal_id) next_animal_id,
                          ─→lead(colour,2) over(order by animal_id) second_next_colour,
                            lead(animal_id,2) over(order by animal_id) second_next_animal_id,
                          ─→lead(colour,3) over(order by animal_id) third_next_colour,
                            lead(animal_id,3) over(order by animal_id) third_next_animal_id
                            FROM anilmal_colour d
                            )
                         WHERE colour          ='Red'
                         AND next_colour       ='Blue'
                         AND second_next_colour='Green'
                         AND third_next_colour ='Yellow'
                         )
                         CONNECT BY regexp_substr(animal_ids_str,'[^,]+',1,level) IS NOT NULL
                    );
                                  ↑
```

This give next colour, for this case Blue

This give 2nd next colur, for this case Green

This give 3rd next colour, for this case Yellow

This will display all the ids in unpivoted rows

The output will be:

ANIMAL_ID	COLOUR
10	Red
11	Blue
12	Green
13	Yellow

Scenario 1: Approach 2: Using MATCH_RECOGNIZE clause in 12c

Using Oracle match_recognize it is fairly simple.

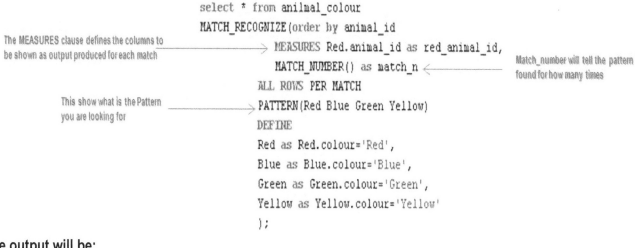

The output will be:

ANIMAL_ID	RED_ANIMAL_ID	MATCH_N	COLOUR
10	10	1	Red
11	10	1	Blue
12	10	1	Green
13	10	1	Yellow

Scenario 2: Find the rows with same flags for 3 consecutive times

Scenario 2: Approach 1: Using Analytical function

Example:

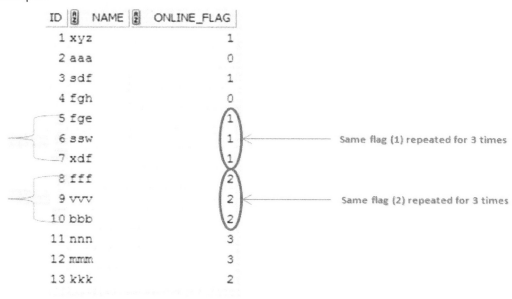

So for this case the pattern is seen in ids [5,6,7] and ids [8,9,10]
Prior to 12c you need to use an analytic function to achieve this

```
create table dc_customer(id number,name varchar2(30),online_flag number);
insert into dc_customer values(1,'xyz',1);
insert into dc_customer values(2,'aaa',0);
insert into dc_customer values(3,'sdf',1);
insert into dc_customer values(4,'fgh',0);
insert into dc_customer values(5,'fge',1);
insert into dc_customer values(6,'ssw',1);
insert into dc_customer values(7,'xdf',1);
insert into dc_customer values(8,'fff',2);
insert into dc_customer values(9,'vvv',2);
insert into dc_customer values(10,'bbb',2);
insert into dc_customer values(11,'nnn',3);
insert into dc_customer values(12,'mmm',3);
insert into dc_customer values(13,'kkk',2);
```

The analytic query to get the pattern:

```
SELECT *
FROM dc_customer
WHERE (id) IN
    (SELECT regexp_substr(cust_ids_str,'[^,]+',1,level)    <--- This will display all the ids in unpivoted rows
    FROM
      (SELECT id
        ||','
        ||next_id
        ||','
        ||second_next_id as cust_ids_str
          FROM
        (SELECT d.*,
          lead(online_flag) over(order by id) next_online_flag,     <-- This give next consecutive flag
          lead(id) over(order by id) next_id,
          lead(online_flag,2) over(order by id) second_next_online_flag,     <-- This give 2nd next consecutive flag
          lead(id,2) over(order by id) second_next_id
        FROM dc_customer d
        )
      where online_flag=next_online_flag      <--- This make sure 3 consecutive flags are same
      and online_flag=second_next_online_flag  <---
      )
    CONNECT BY regexp_substr(cust_ids_str,'[^,]+',1,level) IS NOT NULL
    );
```

The output will be:

60

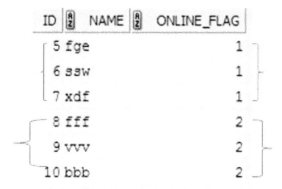

ID	NAME	ONLINE_FLAG
5	fge	1
6	ssw	1
7	xdf	1
8	fff	2
9	vvv	2
10	bbb	2

Scenario 2: Approach 2: Using MATCH_RECOGNIZE clause in 12c

Using Oracle match_recognize it is fairly simple.

```
select * from dc_customer
          MATCH_RECOGNIZE
          (
          order by id
          MEASURES same_flag.online_flag as same_flag_val,
          MATCH_NUMBER() as match_n
          ALL ROWS PER MATCH
          PATTERN(same_flag{3})  <-------- This show pattern is 3 consecutive flag are same
          DEFINE
          same_flag as same_flag.online_flag=first(same_flag.online_flag)
          );
```

The output will be:

ID	SAME_FLAG_VAL	MATCH_N	NAME	ONLINE_FLAG
5	1	1	fge	1
6	1	1	ssw	1
7	1	1	xdf	1
8	2	2	fff	2
9	2	2	vvv	2
10	2	2	bbb	2

Now if you want to find the pattern where 4 consecutive flags are the same then just use this:

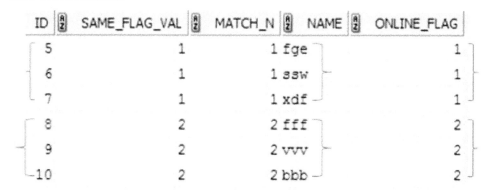

```
PATTERN(same_flag{4})  <----------This show pattern is 4 consecutive flag are same
```

Now for our example four consecutive IDs with the same flag are not present and hence if you run the query based on same_flag {4} the query won't return any output.

Here we will demonstrate how to convert rows into columns.
We will discuss 2 approaches.

Approach 1: Using PIVOT

Using the 11g PIVOT function you can convert rows into columns. PIVOT does the conversion based on aggregation,

CUST_ID	PROPERTY_ID
1234	12
1234	13
1234	14
1234	15
1235	120
1236	130
1236	140
1236	150
1237	1400
1237	1500

This cust has 4 properties → 1234 12 / 1234 13 / 1234 14 / 1234 15

This cust has 1 properties → 1235 120

This cust has 3 properties → 1236 130 / 1236 140 / 1236 150

This cust has 2 properties → 1237 1400 / 1237 1500

Example:

```
CREATE TABLE CUST_PROPERTY
  (
    CUST_ID       NUMBER,
    PROPERTY_ID VARCHAR2(100)
  );

INSERT INTO CUST_PROPERTY VALUES(1234,'12');
INSERT INTO CUST_PROPERTY VALUES(1234,'13');
INSERT INTO CUST_PROPERTY VALUES(1234,'14');
INSERT INTO CUST_PROPERTY VALUES(1234,'15');
INSERT INTO CUST_PROPERTY VALUES(1235,'120');
INSERT INTO CUST_PROPERTY VALUES(1236,'130');
INSERT INTO CUST_PROPERTY VALUES(1236,'140');
INSERT INTO CUST_PROPERTY VALUES(1236,'150');
INSERT INTO CUST_PROPERTY VALUES(1237,'1400');
INSERT INTO CUST_PROPERTY VALUES(1237,'1500');
COMMIT;
```

In this solution you need to use inline view to partition the records based on cust_id and then PIVOT the result.

```
SELECT *
FROM
  (SELECT cust_id,
    PROPERTY_ID,
    row_number() over(partition BY cust_id order by PROPERTY_ID DESC) RN
  FROM CUST_PROPERTY
  )
  PIVOT( MAX(PROPERTY_ID)
  FOR RN IN(1 property_1,2 property_2,3 property_3,4 property_4) );
```

Output:

CUST_ID	PROPERTY_1	PROPERTY_2	PROPERTY_3	PROPERTY_4
1234 15	14	13	12	
1235 120	(null)	(null)	(null)	
1236 150	140	130	(null)	
1237 1500	1400	(null)	(null)	

Approach 2: Without Using PIVOT

Prior to 11g you cannot use PIVOT and hence the solution is as explained:
After aggregating the data using XMLAGG the result-set can be broken down to column level using decode/case, however that approach is very tedious and requires huge effort but with REGEXP_SUBSTR you can achieve the result neatly as below.

```
SELECT cust_id,
  regexp_substr(list_prop,'[^,]+',1,1) AS property_1 ,
  regexp_substr(list_prop,'[^,]+',1,2) AS property_2 ,
  regexp_substr(list_prop,'[^,]+',1,3) AS property_3 ,
  regexp_substr(list_prop,'[^,]+',1,4) AS property_4
FROM
  (SELECT cust_id,
    rtrim(xmlagg(xmlelement(P,property_id
    ||',')).extract('//text()'),',') list_prop
  FROM
    (SELECT DISTINCT cust_id,property_id FROM CUST_PROPERTY ORDER BY cust_id
    )P
  GROUP BY cust_id
  )x;
```

The result will look as below:

CUST_ID	PROPERTY_1	PROPERTY_2	PROPERTY_3	PROPERTY_4
1234 12	15	14	13	
1235 120	(null)	(null)	(null)	
1236 130	150	140	(null)	
1237 1400	1500	(null)	(null)	

So it is possible to dynamically view the rows as any number of columns based on how many property are associated with a cust_id.

In 11g you can use LISTAGG as below:

Now, if you want to display all the property_1, property_2, property_3 etc. <u>in a certain order</u> you can do it using the LISTAGG (introduced in oracle 11g) analytic function for string aggregation as below:

```
SELECT cust_id,
    regexp_substr(list_prop,'[^,]+',1,1) AS property_1 ,
    regexp_substr(list_prop,'[^,]+',1,2) AS property_2 ,
    regexp_substr(list_prop,'[^,]+',1,3) AS property_3 ,
    regexp_substr(list_prop,'[^,]+',1,4) AS property_4
FROM
    (SELECT DISTINCT cust_id,
    LISTAGG(property_id,',') WITHIN GROUP (
    ORDER BY property_id DESC) OVER(partition BY cust_id)list_prop
    FROM
        (SELECT DISTINCT cust_id,property_id FROM CUST_PROPERTY ORDER BY cust_id
        )P
    )x;
```

This clause pivot the rows → LISTAGG(property_id,',') WITHIN GROUP (

This clause sort the pivoted column

This clause group the data

I have seen **approach 1** is faster, however you must try both approach for your scenarios.

Advice 34: Find Top N records using row limiting clause in 12c **OR** normal query **OR** analytical query.

In this tips we will explore **3 approaches** get top N rows from a table. In other words we will explore how pagination is done in oracle.
Here is the setup:

```
CREATE TABLE EMP
  (
    EMPLOYEE_ID    NUMBER(4,0),
    EMPLOYEE_NAME  VARCHAR2(10 BYTE),
    JOB            VARCHAR2(9 BYTE),
    MANAGER_ID     NUMBER(4,0),
    HIREDATE       DATE,
    SAL          NUMBER(7,2),
    COMMISSION     NUMBER(7,2),
    DEPARTMENT_ID  NUMBER(2,0)
  );
```

64

```
Insert into EMP (EMPLOYEE_ID,EMPLOYEE_NAME,JOB,MANAGER_ID,HIREDATE,SAL,COMMISSION,DEPARTMENT_ID)
values (7369,'SMITH','CLERK',7902,to_date('17-DEC-80','DD-MON-RR'),800,null,20);
Insert into EMP (EMPLOYEE_ID,EMPLOYEE_NAME,JOB,MANAGER_ID,HIREDATE,SAL,COMMISSION,DEPARTMENT_ID)
values (7499,'ALLEN','SALESMAN',7698,to_date('20-FEB-81','DD-MON-RR'),1600,300,30);
Insert into EMP (EMPLOYEE_ID,EMPLOYEE_NAME,JOB,MANAGER_ID,HIREDATE,SAL,COMMISSION,DEPARTMENT_ID)
values (7521,'WARD','SALESMAN',7698,to_date('22-FEB-81','DD-MON-RR'),1250,500,30);
Insert into EMP (EMPLOYEE_ID,EMPLOYEE_NAME,JOB,MANAGER_ID,HIREDATE,SAL,COMMISSION,DEPARTMENT_ID)
values (7566,'JONES','MANAGER',7839,to_date('02-APR-81','DD-MON-RR'),2975,null,20);
Insert into EMP (EMPLOYEE_ID,EMPLOYEE_NAME,JOB,MANAGER_ID,HIREDATE,SAL,COMMISSION,DEPARTMENT_ID)
values (7654,'MARTIN','SALESMAN',7698,to_date('28-SEP-81','DD-MON-RR'),1250,1400,30);
Insert into EMP (EMPLOYEE_ID,EMPLOYEE_NAME,JOB,MANAGER_ID,HIREDATE,SAL,COMMISSION,DEPARTMENT_ID)
values (7698,'BLAKE','MANAGER',7839,to_date('01-MAY-81','DD-MON-RR'),2850,null,30);
Insert into EMP (EMPLOYEE_ID,EMPLOYEE_NAME,JOB,MANAGER_ID,HIREDATE,SAL,COMMISSION,DEPARTMENT_ID)
values (7782,'CLARK','MANAGER',7839,to_date('09-JUN-81','DD-MON-RR'),2450,null,10);
Insert into EMP (EMPLOYEE_ID,EMPLOYEE_NAME,JOB,MANAGER_ID,HIREDATE,SAL,COMMISSION,DEPARTMENT_ID)
values (7788,'SCOTT','ANALYST',7566,to_date('19-APR-87','DD-MON-RR'),3000,null,20);
Insert into EMP (EMPLOYEE_ID,EMPLOYEE_NAME,JOB,MANAGER_ID,HIREDATE,SAL,COMMISSION,DEPARTMENT_ID)
values (7839,'KING','PRESIDENT',null,to_date('17-NOV-81','DD-MON-RR'),5000,null,10);
Insert into EMP (EMPLOYEE_ID,EMPLOYEE_NAME,JOB,MANAGER_ID,HIREDATE,SAL,COMMISSION,DEPARTMENT_ID)
values (7844,'TURNER','SALESMAN',7698,to_date('08-SEP-81','DD-MON-RR'),1500,0,30);
Insert into EMP (EMPLOYEE_ID,EMPLOYEE_NAME,JOB,MANAGER_ID,HIREDATE,SAL,COMMISSION,DEPARTMENT_ID)
values (7876,'ADAMS','CLERK',7788,to_date('23-MAY-87','DD-MON-RR'),1100,null,20);
Insert into EMP (EMPLOYEE_ID,EMPLOYEE_NAME,JOB,MANAGER_ID,HIREDATE,SAL,COMMISSION,DEPARTMENT_ID)
values (7900,'JAMES','CLERK',7698,to_date('03-DEC-81','DD-MON-RR'),950,null,30);
Insert into EMP (EMPLOYEE_ID,EMPLOYEE_NAME,JOB,MANAGER_ID,HIREDATE,SAL,COMMISSION,DEPARTMENT_ID)
values (7902,'FORD','ANALYST',7566,to_date('03-DEC-81','DD-MON-RR'),3000,null,20);
Insert into EMP (EMPLOYEE_ID,EMPLOYEE_NAME,JOB,MANAGER_ID,HIREDATE,SAL,COMMISSION,DEPARTMENT_ID)
values (7934,'MILLER','CLERK',7782,to_date('23-JAN-82','DD-MON-RR'),1300,null,10);
COMMIT;
```

Approach 1: Normal query:

```
SELECT * FROM
  ( SELECT * FROM emp ORDER BY sal DESC
  ) WHERE rownum<11;
```

Approach 2: Analytical query:

```
select * from
(
select a.*,row_number() over (order by sal desc) rn from emp a
)
where rn=1;
```

Approach 3: Row limiting clause:

Basic Syntax for TOP N query using ROW limiting clause in 12c:
```
[ OFFSET offset { ROW | ROWS } ]
[ FETCH { FIRST | NEXT } [ { rowcount | percent PERCENT } ]
    { ROW | ROWS } { ONLY | WITH TIES } ]
```

So to get top 10 rows just run:
```
SELECT * FROM emp ORDER BY SAL DESC
FETCH FIRST 10 ROWS ONLY;
```

EMPLOYEE_ID	EMPLOYEE_NAME	JOB	MANAGER_ID	HIREDATE	SAL	COMMISSION	DEPARTMENT_ID
7839 KING	PRESIDENT		(null)	17-NOV-81	5000	(null)	10
7788 SCOTT	ANALYST		7566	19-APR-87	3000	(null)	20
7902 FORD	ANALYST		7566	03-DEC-81	3000	(null)	20
7566 JONES	MANAGER		7839	02-APR-81	2975	(null)	20
7698 BLAKE	MANAGER		7839	01-MAY-81	2850	(null)	30
7782 CLARK	MANAGER		7839	09-JUN-81	2450	(null)	10
7499 ALLEN	SALESMAN		7698	20-FEB-81	1600	300	30
7844 TURNER	SALESMAN		7698	08-SEP-81	1500	0	30
7934 MILLER	CLERK		7782	23-JAN-82	1300	(null)	10
7521 WARD	SALESMAN		7698	22-FEB-81	1250	500	30

If there are duplicate salary values then you can still receive them using "WITH TIES" clause. WITH TIES clause will return more rows if Nth rows value is duplicate. For this case 10th rows SAL is 1250 and this is duplicate and hence return more rows:

```
SELECT * FROM emp ORDER BY SAL DESC
FETCH FIRST 10 rows
WITH TIES;
```

EMPLOYEE_ID	EMPLOYEE_NAME	JOB	MANAGER_ID	HIREDATE	SAL	COMMISSION	DEPARTMENT_ID
7839 KING	PRESIDENT		(null)	17-NOV-81	5000	(null)	10
7788 SCOTT	ANALYST		7566	19-APR-87	3000	(null)	20
7902 FORD	ANALYST		7566	03-DEC-81	3000	(null)	20
7566 JONES	MANAGER		7839	02-APR-81	2975	(null)	20
7698 BLAKE	MANAGER		7839	01-MAY-81	2850	(null)	30
7782 CLARK	MANAGER		7839	09-JUN-81	2450	(null)	10
7499 ALLEN	SALESMAN		7698	20-FEB-81	1600	300	30
7844 TURNER	SALESMAN		7698	08-SEP-81	1500	0	30
7934 MILLER	CLERK		7782	23-JAN-82	1300	(null)	10
7521 WARD	SALESMAN		7698	22-FEB-81	1250	500	30
7654 MARTIN	SALESMAN		7698	28-SEP-81	1250	1400	30

In order to get top 10% of salary records from EMP table:

```
SELECT * FROM emp ORDER BY SAL DESC
FETCH FIRST 10 PERCENT ROWS ONLY;
```

In order to get 6th to 10th records from top 10 salaried records:

```
SELECT * FROM emp ORDER BY SAL DESC OFFSET 5 ROWS
FETCH NEXT 5 ROWS ONLY;
```

OFFSET 5 means skip first 5 records.

The output:

EMPLOYEE_ID	EMPLOYEE_NAME	JOB	MANAGER_ID	HIREDATE	SAL	COMMISSION	DEPARTMENT_ID
7782 CLARK	MANAGER		7839	09-JUN-81	2450	(null)	10
7499 ALLEN	SALESMAN		7698	20-FEB-81	1600	300	30
7844 TURNER	SALESMAN		7698	08-SEP-81	1500	0	30
7934 MILLER	CLERK		7782	23-JAN-82	1300	(null)	10
7521 WARD	SALESMAN		7698	22-FEB-81	1250	500	30

<u>Note:</u> All the above SQL can be directly used in PL/SQL

E.g.

```
DECLARE
   Type t_sal IS TABLE OF emp.sal%type INDEX BY BINARY INTEGER;
   v_sal t_sal;
BEGIN
   SELECT sal bulk collect INTO v_sal FROM emp ORDER BY sal DESC OFFSET 5 ROWS
   FETCH NEXT 5 ROWS only;
END;
/
```

However in this example if you use bind variable (i.e. in DECLARE section add bind_nr number :=5; and in BEGIN section instead of "5 ROWS" use "bind_nr ROWS") , it will fail with error because of oracle bug in 12c (Bug is related with datatype), when used in "OFFSET/FETCH NEXT" clause. The possible workaround is as below:
Use to_number(bind_nr) ROWS instead of bind_nr ROWS [5 ROWS] in the above PL/SQL block.

Advice 35: Get flashback version data for a duration using TIMESTAMP *OR* SCN

To get version data for a duration we have two approaches:

Approach 1: Flashback version query using SCN
We have test11 table which has got flashback enabled. Here is the steps to get the data for a particular period:
Step 1:
Get the SCN number for the particulat timestamp as below:
```
SELECT
timestamp_to_scn(TO_TIMESTAMP('11-12-2016 18:00:00','DD-MM-YYYY HH24:MI:SS')),
timestamp_to_scn(TO_TIMESTAMP('12-12-2016 18:00:00','DD-MM-YYYY HH24:MI:SS'))
FROM dual;
```

TIMESTAMP_TO_SCN(TO_TIMESTAMP('11-12-201618:00:00','DD-MM-YYYYHH24:MI:SS'))	TIMESTAMP_TO_SCN(TO_TIMESTAMP('12-12-201618:00:00','DD-MM-YYYYHH24:MI:SS'))
5834998	5917720

Step 2:
Run the version query:
```
SELECT VERSIONS_STARTTIME,
   versions_operation,
   versions_startscn,
   versions_endscn,
   test11.*
FROM test11 VERSIONS BETWEEN SCN 5834998 AND 5917720
WHERE versions_startscn>= 5834998
AND versions_startscn   <5917720;
```

Approach 2: Flashback version query using Timestamp

```
SELECT VERSIONS_STARTTIME,
  versions_operation,
  versions_startscn,
  versions_endscn,
  test11.*
FROM test11 VERSIONS BETWEEN TIMESTAMP
TO_TIMESTAMP('11-12-2016 18:00:00','DD-MM-YYYY HH24:MI:SS') AND
TO_TIMESTAMP('12-12-2016 18:00:00','DD-MM-YYYY HH24:MI:SS')
WHERE versions_starttime>=
TO_TIMESTAMP('11-12-2016 18:00:00','DD-MM-YYYY HH24:MI:SS') AND
versions_starttime
<TO_TIMESTAMP('12-12-2016 18:00:00','DD-MM-YYYY HH24:MI:SS');
```

Approach 1 i.e. SCN based approach takes less time and henece preferable.

Approach1 is faster because
With the large table data (approx. 100000) and the request for a timestamp based flashback query (using version between TIMESTAMP approach 2) Oracle has to convert the timestamp to an SCN based on the filter used in "where" clause.
So in this case the between clause is returning over 100000 records and calling the conversion for each record and this slows down the performance.

However (using approach 1 version between SCN) the SCN approach no conversion is required and the query is returned immediately.

Advice 36: Normal query OR Sub query factoring using "WITH" clause

Here we will discuss how to reuse a query to avoid re-execution multiple times, instead execute one time and use the result multiple times.

Till Oracle 10gR2 we have seen using WITH clause gives huge performance benefit.
Here is a query which used to take 4 hrs. Now it takes hardly 1 minute to execute.

Approach 1: Normal recursive query
Here is a code snippet

```
SELECT PO_ID,
  TO_CHAR(sysdate, 'DD/Mon/YYYY HH24:MI:SS') AS "Current_Time",
  ERR_CODE,
  FILE_NAME,
  TIME_RECEIVED,
  DATE_RECEIVED,
  NET_SETT_AMT,
  SETTLER,
  SENDER,
  ERR_TYPE,
  ERR_RECORD_TYPE,
  COUNT (err_code) AS err_count
FROM r_validation_errs_v r
WHERE r.po_id                    = NVL (NULL, r.po_id)
AND TRUNC (r.po_date_created) >= NVL (NULL, TRUNC (r.po_date_created))
AND TRUNC (r.po_date_created) <= NVL (NULL, TRUNC (r.po_date_created))
AND r.err_type                   = 'non-critical'
AND r.file_name NOT          IN
  (SELECT c.file_name FROM r_validation_errs_v c WHERE c.err_type = 'critical'
  )
GROUP BY PO_ID,
  ERR_CODE,
  FILE_NAME,
  TIME_RECEIVED,
  DATE_RECEIVED,
  NET_SETT_AMT,
  SETTLER,
  SENDER,
  ERR_TYPE,
  ERR_RECORD_TYPE
ORDER BY FILE_NAME,
  ERR_CODE;
```

This query took some 4 hrs. In Oracle 10g, Please note the view r_validation_errs_v is based on six tables and there are complex joins involved.

Approach 2: Sub query factoring

The WITH clause is referred to as the sub query factoring clause. This clause lets oracle reuse a query when it occurs more than once within the same statement. So instead of storing the query results in a temporary table and performing queries against this temporary table, you can use the WITH clause. By doing this you can avoid a reread and re-execution of the query which in-turn improves overall query execution time and resource utilization. You most frequently use this type of query when querying against large volumes of data e.g. data warehouse.

Now when the query is re-written using the "WITH" clause as below (Temporary table sub query), it took less than 1 minute to execute.

69

```sql
WITH groupings AS
  (SELECT
    /*+ USE_HASH_AGGREGATION */
    PO_ID,
    TO_CHAR(sysdate, 'DD/Mon/YYYY HH24:MI:SS') AS "Current_Time",
    ERR_CODE,
    FILE_NAME,
    TIME_RECEIVED,
    DATE_RECEIVED,
    NET_SETT_AMT,
    SETTLER,
    SENDER,
    ERR_TYPE,
    ERR_RECORD_TYPE,
    COUNT (err_code) AS err_count
  FROM r_validation_errs_v r
  WHERE r.po_id                 = NVL (NULL, r.po_id)
  AND TRUNC (r.po_date_created) >= NVL (NULL, TRUNC (r.po_date_created))
  AND TRUNC (r.po_date_created) <= NVL (NULL, TRUNC (r.po_date_created))
  AND r.err_type                = 'non-critical'
  AND r.file_name NOT           IN
    (SELECT c.file_name FROM r_validation_errs_v c WHERE c.err_type = 'critical'
    )
  GROUP BY PO_ID,
    ERR_CODE,
    FILE_NAME,
    TIME_RECEIVED,
    DATE_RECEIVED,
    NET_SETT_AMT,
    SETTLER,
    SENDER,
    ERR_TYPE,
    ERR_RECORD_TYPE
  )
SELECT * FROM groupings ORDER BY FILE_NAME, ERR_CODE;
```

Please note you should not take this as a rule of thumb and change all queries to use WITH clause (temporary table). Performance is an iterative process and hence you should apply all the refactoring techniques and check the explain plan before deciding which technique is best for your database.
So it is better we acquaint ourselves with all the refactoring techniques and choose the one which is most fitted for each situation.

The performance improvement is realized because of 2 reasons:
1. Use of use_hash_aggregation hint which enforce HASH GROUP BY instead of the costly SORT GROUP BY in the execution plan
2. Sub query refactoring using "WITH" clause which eleminate reread and re-execution of the query and enhance performance.

Here we will discuss different ways to pivot <u>all columns in a table</u>.

As discussed in earlier advice, we can convert rows (for a single column) into columns using **Pivot** and without **pivot** (by using LISTAGG and then break the string using REGEXP_SUBSTR).

Here we will explore how to pivot rows (<u>for all columns</u>) into columns.

Take one example:
```
CREATE TABLE cust_house_det
  (
    cust_id          NUMBER,
    house_no         NUMBER,
    area             NUMBER(14,4),
    registered_flag  NUMBER
  );
INSERT INTO cust_house_det(cust_id,house_no,area,registered_flag) values(1234,12,1371.5,1);
INSERT INTO cust_house_det(cust_id,house_no,area,registered_flag) values(1234,13,1471.5,0);
INSERT INTO cust_house_det(cust_id,house_no,area,registered_flag) values(1234,14,1571.5,0);
```
The data look as below:

CUST_ID	HOUSE_NO	AREA	REGISTERED_FLAG
1234	12	1371.5	1
1234	13	1471.5	0
1234	14	1571.5	0

Objective:
Pivot the whole 3 rows into 1 row.

Approach 1: Using PIVOT:

Using Pivot
```
WITH t1 AS
  (SELECT cust_id,
    house_no,
    area,
    registered_flag,
    row_number() over(partition BY cust_id order by rownum) AS rn
  FROM cust_house_det
  WHERE cust_id=1234
  )
SELECT *
FROM t1
PIVOT( MAX(house_no) AS house_no,MAX(area) AS area, MAX(registered_flag)
AS registered_flag FOR rn IN(1,2,3)
);
```

The output:

CUST_ID	1_HOUSE_NO	1_AREA	1_REGISTERED_FLAG	2_HOUSE_NO	2_AREA	2_REGISTERED_FLAG	3_HOUSE_NO	3_AREA	3_REGISTERED_FLAG
1234	12	1371.5	1	13	1471.5	0	14	1571.5	0

Approach 2: Using normal subquery:

```
SELECT x.cust_id,
  x.house_no house_no_1,
  x.area area_1,
  x.registered_flag registered_flag_1,
  y.house_no house_no_2,
  y.area area_2,
  y.registered_flag registered_flag_2,
  z.house_no house_no_3,
  z.area area_3,
  z.registered_flag registered_flag_3
FROM
  (SELECT *
  FROM
    (SELECT cust_id,
      house_no,
      area,
      registered_flag,
      row_number() over(partition BY cust_id order by house_no DESC) AS rn
    FROM cust_house_det
    WHERE cust_id=1234
    )
  WHERE rn=1
  )x,
  (SELECT *
  FROM
    (SELECT cust_id,
      house_no,
      area,
      registered_flag,
      row_number() over(partition BY cust_id order by house_no DESC) AS rn
    FROM cust_house_det
    WHERE cust_id=1234
    )
  WHERE rn=2
  )y,
  (SELECT *
  FROM
    (SELECT cust_id,
      house_no,
      area,
      registered_flag,
      row_number() over(partition BY cust_id order by house_no DESC) AS rn
    FROM cust_house_det
    WHERE cust_id=1234
    )
  WHERE rn=3
  )z
WHERE x.cust_id=y.cust_id
AND x.cust_id  =z.cust_id;
```

72

The output:

CUST_ID	HOUSE_NO_1	AREA_1	REGISTERED_FLAG_1	HOUSE_NO_2	AREA_2	REGISTERED_FLAG_2	HOUSE_NO_3	AREA_3	REGISTERED_FLAG_3
1234	14	1571.5	0	13	1471.5	0	12	1371.5	1

Approach 3: Using multiple WITH clause

Using "WITH" clause . This gives the great performance (as compared to approach 2) as oracle materializes the temporary tables that are created inside the "WITH" clause.

```
WITH t1 AS
  (SELECT *
  FROM
    (SELECT cust_id,house_no,area,registered_flag,
      row_number() over(partition BY cust_id order by house_no DESC) AS rn
    FROM cust_house_det WHERE cust_id=1234
    )
  WHERE rn=1
  ),
t2 AS
  (SELECT *
  FROM
    (SELECT cust_id,house_no,area,registered_flag,
      row_number() over(partition BY cust_id order by house_no DESC) AS rn
    FROM cust_house_det WHERE cust_id=1234
    )
  WHERE rn=2
  ) ,
t3 AS
  (SELECT *
  FROM
    (SELECT cust_id,house_no,area,registered_flag,
      row_number() over(partition BY cust_id order by house_no DESC) AS rn
    FROM cust_house_det WHERE cust_id=1234
    )
  WHERE rn=3
  )
SELECT
t1.cust_id,t1.house_no house_no_1,t1.area area_1,
t1.registered_flag registered_flag_1,t2.house_no house_no_2,
t2.area area_2,t2.registered_flag registered_flag_2,
t3.house_no house_no_3,t3.area area_3,t3.registered_flag registered_flag_3
FROM t1,t2,t3
WHERE t1.cust_id=t2.cust_id
AND   t1.cust_id=t3.cust_id;
```

The output:

CUST_ID	HOUSE_NO_1	AREA_1	REGISTERED_FLAG_1	HOUSE_NO_2	AREA_2	REGISTERED_FLAG_2	HOUSE_NO_3	AREA_3	REGISTERED_FLAG_3
1234	14	1571.5	0	13	1471.5	0	12	1371.5	1

All the three temp tables have same cust_id value but different area,house_no,registered_flag etc.
Using "WITH" clause you can see the result of temporary tables t1, t2 and t3 have been placed in single row. This is very handy in many scenarios where you must get multiple rows output in a single row.

73

I have shown the example for one "CUST_ID" if you remove the "WHERE CUST_ID=1234" clause the above query will work for all the records in your table.

Out of the 3 approaches, **approach 1** is most favorable in terms of coding/maintainance and performance.

Advice 38: Oracle Object CACHE Using "Cache" *OR* "Keep buffer pool" *OR* Oracle 12c "IN-MEMORY column store"

Here we will discuss different ways of pinning an object (or part of the object) in memory for better performance.

When you run a query multiple times in the same session the response time reduces because blocks are cached and, as per LRU algorithm, are subsequently aged out of the cache block. Caching means pinning the data.
So when you talk about "Caching object" it means you PIN the object in memory. So here we will discuss 3 different ways of Caching using a simple example

Approach 1: using Cache
```
alter table t1 cache;
```
In this approach you will pin a frequently used small table in memory. But in real sense this is not fully in memory. The table is kept in general buffer cache but it stays at the most recently used end of LRU list, that means it is not susceptible to being aged out of cache very frequently. It stays in the cache longer but based on system demand it is aged out for sure sooner or later. Here the full table is pinned even if you need some section of the table to be pinned

Approach 2: using keep buffer pool
```
alter table t1 storage (buffer_pool Keep);
```
In this approach also you will pin a frequently used small table in memory. Here the table is placed in the special section of the cache called the KEEP buffer pool and hence the table is never aged out from the cache. Here the full table is pinned even if you need some section of the table to be pinned.

Approach 3: using IN-MEMORY column store
In-memory Column-store (IM-COLUMN) is a mechanism (introduced in Oracle 12c) by which performance critical subset of a table is placed in the "in-memory column store" which is the new section of the SGA in Oracle 12c. This "in-memory area" can be configured using "INMEMORY_SIZE" initialization parameter. You can store whole table, set of columns, specific group of columns, materialized view, table partition etc. in the IM-COLUMN store.
In-memory storage not only helps accessing data in memory (approach 1 and approach 2 which are based fundamentally on accessing data from memory cache only) it helps reporting, business intelligence and high performance analytical queries run faster by its internal algorithm to keep the data in columnar format instead of traditional row format.

Example how to configure:

```
ALTER SYSTEM SET SGA_TARGET=4G SCOPE=SPFILE;
ALTER SYSTEM SET INMEMORY_SIZE=2G SCOPE=SPFILE;  <─────  Enabling the IN-MEMORY
SHUTDOWN IMMEDIATE;
STARTUP;
```

```
ALTER SYSTEM SET INMEMORY_SIZE=0;  <─────────  Disabling the IN-MEMORY SYSTEM level
ALTER SESSION SET INMEMORY_SIZE=0;  <
SHUTDOWN IMMEDIATE;                             Disabling the IN-MEMORY SESSION level
STARTUP;
```

Example how to use IM-COLUMN store (IMDB in short):

```
CREATE TABLE t1
   (
      id NUMBER,
      a  NUMBER,
      b  NUMBER,
      c  NUMBER,
      d  NUMBER,
      e  NUMBER,
      f  NUMBER
   )
   INMEMORY;  <─────────  This clause keep the table in IMDB
```

In-memory (IM) setting for this table can be changed as below:

```
ALTER TABLE t1 NO INMEMORY;  <──────────  Table out of IMDB

ALTER TABLE t1 INMEMORY;  <──────────  Full Table in IMDB

ALTER TABLE t1  NO INMEMORY(b,c,d);  <──────  Only b, c, d columns are out of IMDB

ALTER TABLE t1  INMEMORY(b,c);  <──────  b, c, columns are again in IMDB
```

For materialized view the command is:

```
CREATE MATERIALIZED VIEW t1_mview INMEMORY
AS SELECT * FROM t1;
```

As per Oracle documentation:

IM column store is good in the following scenarios:

- Large scans using "=", "<", ">" and "IN" filters, IN-MEMORY join use bloom filter.
- When it selects few columns from a table with large number of columns.
- Join small tables to large tables.
- In-memory aggregation.

IM column store is not good in the following scenarios:

- Complex predicates in the join
- Join returning large set of columns and large number of rows.
- Join large table to large table.

75

Approach 3 gives tremendous performance as compared to **approach 1** and **approach 2**

However you must weigh all the options before finalizing the solution for different scenarios.

Advice 39: Result cache function *OR* No Cache function *OR* deterministic function *OR* PL/SQL collection

In oracle there are different ways to store a value in memory and implement complex logic. Here we will discuss different approaches to do that.

Approach 1: Function result-cached:

This is a function whose argument values and corresponding result-set are stored in the cache in SGA area. Function result cache is mostly used when the function contain lots of complex sql query inside it. In oracle 11g PL/SQL function result cache is <u>cross session result cache</u>.

```
CREATE OR REPLACE FUNCTION f2_result_cache(
                p_first_name IN VARCHAR2
                ) RETURN VARCHAR2
                  RESULT_CACHE
                  RELIES_ON (cust)
                IS
                v_id_name varchar2(60);
    BEGIN
        select upper(id||'-'||last_name) INTO v_id_name from cust
        where first_name=p_first_name and rownum<2;
        RETURN v_id_name;
    END f2_result_cache;
/
```

Now if you execute
```
select first_name,last_name,f2_result_cache(first_name) from cust;
```
It will take approx. 10 sec in my testing even if you run it from different sessions (As result cache is applicable for cross session).

Approach 2: Function NO-cached:
In this approach we use conventional function to return the result.
```
CREATE OR REPLACE FUNCTION f2_no_cache(
                p_first_name IN VARCHAR2
                ) RETURN VARCHAR2
                IS
                v_id_name varchar2(60);
    BEGIN
        select upper(id||'-'||last_name) INTO v_id_name from cust
        where first_name=p_first_name and rownum<2;
        RETURN v_id_name;
    END f2_no_cache;
/
```
You can execute as below:
```
select first_name,last_name,f2_no_cache(first_name) from cust;
```

This takes little longer than 19 sec:

Approach 3: Deterministic Function:

A deterministic function uses the pre-computed result for a specific session.

```
CREATE OR REPLACE FUNCTION f2_deterministic(
                p_first_name IN VARCHAR2
                ) RETURN VARCHAR2 DETERMINISTIC
                IS
                v_id_name varchar2(60);
    BEGIN
        select upper(id||'-'||last_name) INTO v_id_name from cust
        where first_name=p_first_name and rownum<2;
        RETURN v_id_name;
    END f2_deterministic;
/
```

When you execute:
```
select first_name,last_name,f2_deterministic(first_name) from cust;
```

If this is executed 2nd time in same session it takes approx. 10 second as it takes for result cache function (approach 1). However if it is executed in different session it takes around 19 sec.

Approach 4: PL/SQL collection:

PL/SQL collection is similar to array in C. The data of PL/SQL collection is stored in PGA memory and PL/SQL runtime engine can directly access it. Note, this data storage happens in each and every session independently which means cross session interoperability is not there for PL/SQL collection.

As you know PL/SQL function results are stored in SGA (not in PGA) and PL/SQL collection stores the data in PGA. Since getting data from PGA (RAM) is much faster than getting data from SGA we have seen PL/SQL collection is faster than function result cache. *However you have to store the collection result of each session in PGA and hence you may run out of total PGA memory in a multi-user environment. This should be taken into consideration when deciding which approach to use.*

The following example uses PL/SQL collection instead of a function result cache

```
DECLARE
  v_id_name DBMS_SQL.VARCHAR2_TABLE;
  v_first_names DBMS_SQL.VARCHAR2_TABLE;
  v_last_names DBMS_SQL.VARCHAR2_TABLE;
BEGIN
  SELECT first_name,
    last_name,
    upper(id
    ||'-'
    ||last_name) BULK COLLECT
  INTO v_first_names,
    v_last_names,
    v_id_name
  FROM cust;
  FOR i IN 1 .. v_first_names.COUNT
  LOOP
    dbms_output.put_line('v_id_name is:'||v_id_name);
  END LOOP;
END;
/
```

This block will take less than 6 sec to execute.

So in a nutshell:

- o Use function result cache when the function has complex sql logic embedded. The function result cache is referred as a cross session function result cache because it caches the result-set across the sessions.
- o Use function result cache over deterministic when you work in multi user environment where you want to get the benefit of running the same function in different sessions.
- o When it comes to use result cache function or associative array (PL/SQL table) you have seen PL/SQL table(PL/SQL collection) is better than function result cache because PL/SQL table gets the data from PGA and function result cache gets the data from SGA. However there is a trade-off between performance and memory usage.
- o When your underlying table in the function undergoes frequent DML changes then function result cache is not ideal for the function as DML change will force the database to invalidate the result set.
- o Most importantly consider using function result cache if the time spent in specific function business logic is more than time spent in result cache mechanism. If time spent in evaluating the business logic is less than the time spent in evaluating the result cache mechanism it is advisable not to use the result cache. Classic example for this scenario is when you need to concatenate two inputs by comma or do some simple arithmetic on the data. In these kinds of scenario you should not use result cache function.

One more example to demonstrate the performance of no cache, function result cache and deterministic function:

We will create simple function using these 3 methods and show the result after processing all the rows.

78

```
CREATE OR REPLACE FUNCTION fl_result_cache(
                p_first_name IN VARCHAR2,
                p_last_name  IN VARCHAR2
                ) RETURN VARCHAR2
                  RESULT_CACHE
                  RELIES_ON (cust)
                IS
      BEGIN
         RETURN p_first_name || ' ' || p_last_name;
      END fl_result_cache;
/
CREATE OR REPLACE FUNCTION fl_no_cache(
                p_first_name IN VARCHAR2,
                p_last_name  IN VARCHAR2
                ) RETURN VARCHAR2
                   IS
      BEGIN
         RETURN p_first_name || ' ' || p_last_name;
      END fl_no_cache;
/
CREATE OR REPLACE FUNCTION fl_deterministic(
                p_first_name IN VARCHAR2,
                p_last_name  IN VARCHAR2
                ) RETURN VARCHAR2
                  DETERMINISTIC
                  IS
      BEGIN
         RETURN p_first_name || ' ' || p_last_name;
      END fl_deterministic;
/
```

Once these functions are created, we are ready to execute each functions and note down time as show in Below example:

```
set serverout on 20000000
DECLARE
  v_cust_name VARCHAR2(60);
  v_first_names DBMS_SQL.VARCHAR2_TABLE;
  v_last_names DBMS_SQL.VARCHAR2_TABLE;
  v_cnt NUMBER :=1500;
  t1      NUMBER;
  t2      NUMBER;
  t3      NUMBER;
  t4      NUMBER;
BEGIN
  SELECT first_name,
    last_name BULK COLLECT
  INTO v_first_names,
    v_last_names
  FROM cust WHERE rownum<1501;
  t1          :=dbms_utility.get_time;
  FOR i     IN 1 .. v_first_names.COUNT
  LOOP
    FOR j IN 1 .. v_cnt LOOP
      v_cust_name := fl_result_cache( v_first_names(i), v_last_names(i) );
    END LOOP;
  END LOOP;
  t2:=dbms_utility.get_time;
  dbms_output.put_line('time taken to execute with result cache is:'||(t2-t1));
  FOR i                              IN 1 .. v_first_names.COUNT
  LOOP
    FOR j IN 1 .. v_cnt LOOP
      v_cust_name := fl_no_cache( v_first_names(i), v_last_names(i) );
    END LOOP;
  END LOOP;
  t3:=dbms_utility.get_time;
  dbms_output.put_line('time taken to execute with no cache is:'||(t3-t2));
  FOR i                              IN 1 .. v_first_names.COUNT
  LOOP
    FOR j IN 1 .. v_cnt LOOP
      v_cust_name := fl_deterministic( v_first_names(i), v_last_names(i) );
    END LOOP;
  END LOOP;
  t4:=dbms_utility.get_time;
  dbms_output.put_line('TIME taken TO EXECUTE WITH deterministic IS:'||(t4-t3));
END;
/
```

The output is
```
time taken to execute with result cache is:126
time taken to execute with no cache is:90
TIME taken TO EXECUTE
WITH deterministic IS:89
```

So this shows the time spent in evaluating result cache result is more than time spent in evaluating the business logic and hence there is no performance improvement rather we get performance penalty. In fact in this kind of scenario deterministic performs the best.

However consider a scenario as below which has only a few distinct return values (let us say 20-30 values) however this function is used in a view which returns millions of records then you must use result cache function to use the pre-computed value.

So in this case p_type has only 20 distinct values and it returns 20 distinct java.lang.string
However **complex_view** has more than 1 million records based on join on multiple base tables including tab1.

```
create or replace
function fl(p_type in number)
return VARCHAR2
RESULT_CACHE
RELIES ON(tab1)
as language java name 'com.xx.utility.rad50ToString(java.math.BigDecimal)
return java.lang.String';
/
```

So when we fire the following query
```
SELECT id,name,p_type,fl(p_type) FROM complex_view;
```
                This function return 20 distinct name   This View return millions of rows

It does not compute the function f1 more than a million times. Instead it compute only 20 times (by eliminating redundant function calls) and the remaining times it uses the pre-computed result not only in 1 session but across other sessions and gives huge performance benefit.

Here are the restriction on using function result cache:
- It cannot be used in invoker's rights code or in an anonymous block.
- It cannot be used in a pipelined table function.
- It cannot be used in a function which has OUT or IN OUT parameters.
- It cannot be used in a function whose IN parameter has one of the following types,
- BLOB, CLOB, NCLOB, REF CURSOR, Collection Object, Record.
- It cannot be used in a function which has return type BLOB, CLOB, NCLOB, REF CURSOR, Object, Record or PL/SQL collection that contains one of the preceding unsupported return types.

Advice 40: Function result cache *OR* Oracle user Cache *OR* No Cache

Here we will discuss and compare different mechanisms to eliminate the expensive read from kernel/physical disk.

Approach 1: Function result-cache:

This is a function whose argument values and corresponding result-set are stored in the cache in SGA area. Function result cache is mostly used when the function contain lots of complex sql query inside it. In oracle 11g PL/SQL function result cache is cross session result cache.

Approach 2: Function NO-cached:
In this approach we use conventional function to return the result.

Approach 3: Oracle user cache:

Oracle user cache is the mechanism by which a value in an oracle package is stored as a variable and we can retrieve that value from buffer cache which eliminates the expensive read from kernel/physical disk.
Here you will see the Cache mechanism is best when compared with no cache.

However *oracle user cache* is slightly better than *function result cache (This was discussed in earlier Tips).*

```
CREATE OR REPLACE PACKAGE user_cache AS
FUNCTION f2_user_cache(
                p_first_name IN VARCHAR2
                ) RETURN VARCHAR2;
FUNCTION f2_result_cache(
                p_first_name IN VARCHAR2
                ) RETURN VARCHAR2
                  RESULT_CACHE;
                  --RELIES_ON (cust);
FUNCTION f2_no_cache(
                p_first_name IN VARCHAR2
                ) RETURN VARCHAR2;
END user_cache;
/
```

```
CREATE OR REPLACE PACKAGE body user_cache AS
        TYPE user_cache_t IS TABLE OF varchar2(100) INDEX BY varchar2(100);
        g_user_cache user_cache_t;

    FUNCTION f2_user_cache(
                p_first_name IN VARCHAR2
                ) RETURN VARCHAR2
                IS
     BEGIN
     IF NOT g_user_cache.EXISTS(p_first_name) THEN
         select upper(id||'-'||last_name) INTO g_user_cache(p_first_name)
         from cust
         where first_name=p_first_name and rownum<2;
       END IF;
         RETURN g_user_cache(p_first_name);
       END f2_user_cache;

    FUNCTION f2_result_cache(
                p_first_name IN VARCHAR2
                ) RETURN VARCHAR2
                  RESULT_CACHE
                  RELIES_ON (cust)
                IS
                v_id_name varchar2(60);
      BEGIN
         select upper(id||'-'||last_name) INTO v_id_name from cust
         where first_name=p_first_name and rownum<2;
         RETURN v_id_name;
       END f2_result_cache;

    FUNCTION f2_no_cache(
                p_first_name IN VARCHAR2
                ) RETURN VARCHAR2
                IS
                v_id_name varchar2(60);
      BEGIN
         select upper(id||'-'||last_name) INTO v_id_name from cust
         where first_name=p_first_name and rownum<2;
         RETURN v_id_name;
       END f2_no_cache;
END user_cache;
/
```

Now when we execute all the 3 functions from PL/SQL we can see the performance difference as shown:

```
declare
  t1     NUMBER;
  t2     NUMBER;
  t3     NUMBER;
  t4     NUMBER;
  v_id_name varchar2(60);
begin
  t1:=dbms_utility.get_time;
for i in (select first_name from cust) loop
  v_id_name :=user_cache.f2_no_cache(i.first_name);
end loop;
  t2:=dbms_utility.get_time;
dbms_output.put_line('Time taken with no cache:'||(t2-t1));
for i in (select first_name from cust) loop
  v_id_name :=user_cache.f2_result_cache(i.first_name);
end loop;
  t3:=dbms_utility.get_time;
dbms_output.put_line('Time taken with result cache:'||(t3-t2));
for i in (select first_name from cust) loop
  v_id_name :=user_cache.f2_user_cache(i.first_name);
end loop;
  t4:=dbms_utility.get_time;
dbms_output.put_line('Time taken with user cache:'||(t4-t3));
end;
/
```

The output look as below:

```
Time taken with no cache:13513
Time taken with result cache:7375
Time taken with user cache:6654
```

So this suggests Caching is good for performance, for this example Oracle cache is the best. However you should not jump to conclusions, you should consider all the options for your business scenario and finally decide which option is best for you.

Advice 41: Correlated update *OR* merge *OR* different approach to update

Here we will discuss different approaches for "update" to get better performance.
The data looks as below:

```
CREATE TABLE test_s
  (cust_id VARCHAR2(8),house_no NUMBER,buying_date DATE
  );
INSERT INTO test_s VALUES('Asim 01',1,TO_DATE('06-01-2015','DD-MM-YYYY'));
INSERT INTO test_s VALUES('Arun 01',2,TO_DATE('06-01-2015','DD-MM-YYYY'));
INSERT INTO test_s VALUES('Ani 01',3,TO_DATE('06-01-2015','DD-MM-YYYY'));
INSERT INTO test_s VALUES('Aditi 01',44,TO_DATE('06-01-2015','DD-MM-YYYY'));
COMMIT;
```

```
CREATE TABLE test_tgt
  (cust_id VARCHAR2(8),house_no NUMBER,buying_date DATE
  );
INSERT INTO test_tgt VALUES('Asim 01',1,TO_DATE('07-01-2015','DD-MM-YYYY'));
INSERT INTO test_tgt VALUES('Arun 01',2,TO_DATE('07-01-2015','DD-MM-YYYY'));
INSERT INTO test_tgt VALUES('Ani 01',3,TO_DATE('07-01-2015','DD-MM-YYYY'));
INSERT INTO test_tgt VALUES('Aditi 01',44,TO_DATE('07-01-2015','DD-MM-YYYY'));
INSERT INTO test_tgt VALUES('PPPP 01',10,TO_DATE('07-01-2015','DD-MM-YYYY'));
COMMIT;
```

Note cust_id PPPP 01 is not present in table "test_s" however it is present in table "test_tgt".

Now you need to update test_tgt with the value from test_s
Here is the update statement:

```
UPDATE test_tgt a
SET (house_no,buying_date)=(SELECT house_no,buying_date FROM test_s b
WHERE b.cust_id=a.cust_id);
```

Do you find any issue in the update?

This will update the cust_id PPPP 01 in test_tgt with house_no and buying_date as null because this cust_id is not present in test_s source table.

The data in test_tgt look as below after the update.

CUST_ID	HOUSE_NO	BUYING_DATE
Asim 01	1	06-JAN-15
Arun 01	2	06-JAN-15
Ani 01	3	06-JAN-15
Aditi 01	44	06-JAN-15
PPPP 01	(null)	(null)

To resolve this here is the correct update statement:

Approach 1: Using correlated update

```
UPDATE test_tgt a
SET (house_no,buying_date)=(SELECT house_no,buying_date FROM test_s b
WHERE b.cust_id=a.cust_id)
WHERE EXISTS (SELECT 1 FROM test_s c
              WHERE c.cust_id=a.cust_id);
```

However this approach is inefficient because "test_s" table is queried twice.

To resolve the performance issue here are 2 approaches to update the test_tgt table

Approach 2: joined 2 tables
Here we update the joined version of both tables by issuing update on the inline view as below:

However there are some restriction in this approach. You must make sure both the table test_s and test_tgt are joined on primary key column. If the tables are not joined using primary key column it will fail with error

```
UPDATE
  (SELECT a.house_no src_hou,
    a.buying_date src_dt,
    b.house_no tgt_hou,
    b.buying_date tgt_dt
  FROM test_s a,
    test_tgt b
  WHERE a.house_no=b.house_no
  )
SET tgt_hou=src_hou,
  tgt_dt   =src_dt;


SQL Error: ORA-01779: cannot modify a column which maps to a non key-preserved table
01779. 00000 -  "cannot modify a column which maps to a non key-preserved table"
*Cause:     An attempt was made to insert or update columns of a join view which
            map to a non-key-preserved table.
*Action:    Modify the underlying base tables directly.
```

So this approach is used when you have same kind of table or has some backup table of the original table.

Approach 3: merge
We can use Oracle Merge to do this as below:
```
MERGE INTO test_tgt tgt
USING
test_s src
ON (tgt.cust_id=src.cust_id)
WHEN MATCHED THEN
UPDATE SET
tgt.house_no=src.house_no,
tgt.buying_date=src.buying_date;
```

I personally opt for approach 3 because of ease of use, no restriction as seen in approach 2, less amount code and better response time, however it is suggested to try all approaches before deciding on final approach.

Advice 42: Oracle NOT IN OR MINUS OR JOIN OR NOT EXISTS clause
Here we will discuss different ways to refactor a query for better performance.

When you have requirement to derive a set of values from a set of source tables, there are different ways to derive the same result based on the complexity of the requirement.

To demonstrate the relative performance of each method here is a simple example. Please note in order to see considerable difference in performance you need to use a complex query with multiple joins and a minimum 3-4 tables. For a simple query on a small data set, performance will be similar whichever method is chosen. All the methods return the same result but there will be difference in response time. Explain plan will show the reason for the differences.

Approach 1: "NOT IN" method

```
SELECT a.app_id
FROM app a
WHERE a.app_id  =2
AND app_id NOT IN
  (SELECT app_id FROM app_parcel WHERE a.app_id=2
  );
```

This takes approx. 4 seconds (as it does not use the index). In Oracle NOT IN clause trigger the full table scan even if there is index in app_id column.

Note: Oracle does not use index with NOT predicates e.g. NOT IN, NOT LIKE, NOT BETWEEN, <>, NOT >=. Also NULL predicate will not use index. (However for **NOT EXISTS** clause it uses index)

Approach 2: "NOT EXISTS" method

```
SELECT a.app_id
FROM app a
WHERE a.app_id  =2
AND not exists
  (SELECT 1 FROM app_parcel b WHERE b.app_id=a.app_id);
```

This takes approx. 2 seconds as it uses the index.

Approach 3: "JOIN" method

```
SELECT DISTINCT a.app_id
FROM app a,
  app_parcel b
WHERE a.app_id =b.app_id(+)
AND b.app_id  IS NULL;
```

Note here you need to use distinct clause to eliminate the duplicate records,
This takes approx. 6 seconds

Approach 4: "MINUS" method

```
SELECT a.app_id
FROM app a
MINUS
SELECT b.app_id
FROM app_parcel b;
```

This takes approx. 2 seconds

So in a nutshell

1. if your requirement is to display the result irrespective of whether there are any duplicates then it is better to use JOIN or MINUS or NOT EXISTS rather than "NOT IN" clause. MINUS is more preferable.

2. If your requirement is to display the result without duplicates it is better to use NOT IN or NOT EXISTS or MINUS instead of JOIN clause. NOT EXISTS is better than NOT IN. MINUS is most preferable. However you must try all approaches before deciding any specific approach as performance tuning is an iterative process. There is no "one size fits all" solution in Oracle. These are just recommendations.

Advice 43: Nested loop join *OR* Hash join *OR* Parallelism *OR* Multithreading

Here we will discuss different types of internal join methods and option to run your code in multi-threaded mode.

Let us take one example to see the performance of each process

We have 2 tables
Small table is "apps" which has around 60,000 records and
Big table "shop" which has around 1,100,000 records

And after joining the final result-set returns around 162,000 records, please note for this case both tables are almost equally big and hence it is preferable to use HASH join over nested loop join
However we will discuss all the alternate ways to get the resultset.

Approach 1: "Nested loop join" method

Nested loop join is good for small result-set where one table is small and by using index range scan we can derive the final result-set quickly.

```
SELECT /*+ use_nl(S L)*/
S.product_id,L.shop_id
from apps S,shop L
where S.apps_id=L.apps_id
and L.shop_region='ASIA';
```

This takes roughly 20 sec

Approach 2: "Hash join" method

Hash join is good when larger result-set is expected and both the tables are big as using nested loop join for this scenario will require numerous index range scans.

```
SELECT /*+ use_hash(L S)*/
S.product_id,L.shop_id
from apps S,shop L
where S.apps_id=L.apps_id
and L.shop_region='ASIA';
```

This will take roughly 12 sec as expected because for this scenario Hash join is better alternative than nested loop join.

Approach 3: "Parallelism" method

Parallelism can be done on both hash join and nested loop join. It is a mechanism by which multiple process execute the same job. Multiple process creation is determined by degree of parallelism which is discussed in this book.

```
SELECT /*+ PARALLEL(L,6) use_hash(L S)*/
S.product_id,L.shop_id
from apps S,shop L
where S.apps_id=L.apps_id
and L.shop_region='ASIA';
```

This will take roughly 3 sec

Note that here in big table "shop" (alias L) we have imposed the parallelism of degree 6.

Approach 4: "Multithreading" method

Multi-threading is done on nested loop join. It is a mechanism by which multiple process execute the same job. Multiple process creation is determined by degree of parallelism which is discussed in this book.
The difference between parallelism and multi-threading is that parallelism usually involves full table/index scan and multi-threading involves sequential read of single block obviously via index scan.
Let us take one example to see the performance of each process

```
SELECT /*+ PARALLEL(S 30) use_nl(S L)*/
S.product_id,L.shop_id
from apps S,shop L
where S.apps_id=L.apps_id
and L.shop_region='ASIA';
```

This will take roughly 0.2 sec.

Note that here in small table "apps" (alias S) we have imposed the parallelism of degree 30. This is the opposite of what we do in the parallelism (approach 3) where in the big table only we impose parallelism.

This approach 4 (nested loop multi-threading using parallelism) does not work when the query contains "WHERE IN" clause or "WHERE EXISTS" clause because oracle apparently cannot divide the work and coordinate the nested loop slaves.

Also note approach 3 implements parallelism whereas approach 4 implements multi-threading. The difference between parallelism and multi-threading is that parallelism usually involves full table/index scan and multi-threading involves sequential read of single block obviously via index scan. Both approach 3 and 4 uses parallelism but in <u>opposite</u> ways.

Note: One more thing I would like to add on top of the methods mentioned: I have seen that sometimes hash join is better than nested loop join even if it completely fits the nested loop join criteria. E.g. when you use in the where clause "(cola, colb) IN (select x, y from tab...) "oracle uses a nested loop join and takes hours however if you convert this "(cola||colb) IN (select x||y from tab...) "it uses a hash join and finish in few minutes only. Have this trick in your hand and check if it helps in some of your solutions.

As a rule "WHERE" clause is used to filter the normal data and "HAVING" clause is used to filter the <u>grouped data</u> and <u>also to filter normal data</u>. So both are useful in their own way.

However when there is a question to use "WHERE or HAVING" clause to filter data you must make sure you use "WHERE" clause to filter normal data and should not use "HAVING" clause to filter normal data.

Approach 1: Using "HAVING" clause

The "HAVING" clause filters group of rows after they have been grouped. So this grouping operation will take some time to execute and consume some resource. Now if you do not need some grouped data as a matter of understanding one should not group that data in the first place.

For e.g.

```
SELECT deptno,
   COUNT(*)
FROM emp
GROUP BY Deptno
HAVING deptno NOT   IN(2,3)
AND COUNT(        *)>500;
```

In this example you are unnecessarily grouping deptno for deptno in (2, 3) and then in "HAVING" clause you discard the data.

Approach 2: Using "WHERE" clause

To make the query in approach 1, efficient and reduce the overhead of grouping unnecessary deptno you need to first filter the deptno in "WHERE" clause instead of "HAVING" clause.

The restructured query look as below:

```
SELECT deptno,
   COUNT(*)
FROM emp
WHERE deptno NOT IN(2,3)
GROUP BY Deptno
HAVING COUNT(*)>500;
```

The execution path of a query is as follows:
WHERE → GROUP BY → HAVING → ORDER BY
So ensure that filtering activities are executed as early as possible rather than leaving them all to the final "HAVING" step.

This is a very simple tip which is often ignored resulting in a huge performance penalty, especially in an environment where these kinds of query are executed millions of times and hence are resource intensive.

Here we will discuss ways to refactor query to eliminate costly sorting which is incurred when you use "DISTINCT".

From experience we have seen that "EXISTS" is better than "IN". Also many times we can avoid the very expensive "DISTINCT" keyword and use "EXISTS" clause to get the distinct value from Oracle.

You use "IN" clause to check if the value is present in a table or in a data-set whereas you use "EXISTS" clause to check only the existence of row (not any actual data).

You can display the unique value in a table by using "DISTINCT" keyword. The "DISTINCT" keyword internally sorts the retrieved rows (all data) and then removes the duplicates and displays the unique values. This is a very expensive operation. However using "EXISTS" you can display only the distinct values without using "DISTINCT" keyword.

We will check all the 3 examples here
In app table you have all the unique app_id (i.e. product id), let's say you have 10000 app_id

In purchase table you have all the app_id which has been purchased by any customer. So app_id may be present in purchase table more than 1 time or it may not present at all if no one purchased that product. Let us say in purchase you have 100000 records.

Now our objective is to display all the unique product id (app_id) which has been at least purchased by 1 person.

We can achieve this by 3 methods:

Approach 1: Using "IN" method

You use "IN" clause to check if the value is present in a table

```
SELECT app_id FROM app a WHERE app_id IN
  (SELECT app_id FROM purchase b
  );
```

This will take 5 seconds...

Approach 2: Using "EXISTS" method

You use "EXISTS" clause to check only the existence of row (not any actual data).

```
SELECT app_id
FROM app a
WHERE EXISTS
  (SELECT 1 FROM purchase b WHERE b.app_id=a.app_id
  );
```
This will take 1 second...

Approach 3: Using "DISTINCT" method

91

You can display the unique value in a table by using "DISTINCT" keyword. The "DISTINCT" keyword internally sorts the retrieved rows (all data) and then removes the duplicates and displays the unique values. This is a very expensive operation. However using "EXISTS" as per approach 2, you can display only the distinct values without using "DISTINCT" keyword.

```
SELECT DISTINCT a.app_id
FROM app a, purchase b
WHERE a.app_id=b.app_id;
```

This will take 130 seconds...

So it is evident from the example that "EXISTS" is better than "IN" and "DISTINCT" and you know how you can refactor your query to use "EXISTS" instead of the very expensive "DISTINCT" clause in many scenarios.

Advice 46: Oracle clause "IN" OR "EXISTS" OR "INTERSECT" OR "JOIN"

Here we will discuss again more ways to refactor a query for better performance.

When you have requirement to derive a set of values from two or more source tables there are different ways to derive the result based on the complexity of the requirement.

To demonstrate the relative performance of each method here is a simple example. Please note in order to see considerable difference in performance you need to use complex query with multiple joins and a minimum of 3-4 tables. For a simple query it does not make any difference whether you use any of the 4 methods.

Approach 1: Using "IN" method

You use "IN" clause to check if the value is present in a table

```
SELECT a.app_id
FROM app a
WHERE a.app_id=2345
AND app_id   IN
  (SELECT b.app_id FROM app_repository b WHERE b.app_id =2345
  );
```

This takes approx. 3 seconds

Approach 2: Using "EXISTS" method

You use "EXISTS" clause to check only the existence of row (not any actual data).

```
SELECT a.app_id
FROM app a
WHERE a.app_id=2345
AND EXISTS
   (SELECT 1 FROM app_repository b WHERE b.app_id=a.app_id AND b.app_id =2345
   );
```

This takes approx. 1 seconds

Approach 3: Using "JOIN" method

```
SELECT DISTINCT a.app_id
FROM app a,
   app_repository b
WHERE a.app_id=b.app_id
AND a.app_id =2345;
```

Note here you need to use distinct clause to eliminate duplicate records.
This takes approx. 4 seconds

Approach 4: Using "INTERSECT" method

```
SELECT a.app_id FROM app a WHERE a.app_id=2345
INTERSECT
SELECT b.app_id FROM app_repository b WHERE b.app_id=2345;
```

This takes approx. 1 second

From analysis we found instead of using "IN" clause to derive the final set of rows from different sources it is advisable to use JOIN or INTERSECT. However many a time if you use JOIN you need to use DISTINCT keyword to remove the duplicate, but INTERSECT will internally remove the duplicates.

So it is suggested to use a set operator like INTERSECT to combine different criteria and get the result quickly.
So in a nutshell
1. If your requirement is to display the result irrespective of whether there are any duplicates then it is better to use JOIN or INTERSECT rather than "IN" clause. INTERSECT is preferable.
2. If your requirement is to display the result without duplicates it is better to use IN or EXISTS or INTERSECT instead of JOIN clause. INTERSECT is most preferable. However you must try all approaches before deciding which to use as performance tuning is an iterative process. There is no one size fits all solution in Oracle. These are just recommendations.

Advice 47: Oracle clause "OR" *OR* "UNION"

Here we will discuss how to refactor a query to use "UNION" clause instead of "OR" clause to get better performance.

When you want to derive the result from a hierarchical query do not use OR clause as it makes the optimizer use FULL table scan and query performance is affected badly.
In fact Oracle suggest not to use OR clause and their advice is to use UNION instead.

Approach 1: Using "OR" method

```
SELECT *
FROM tabl
WHERE id=6
OR
ID IN
  (SELECT id
  FROM tabl
    START WITH parent_id IN
    (SELECT id FROM tabl WHERE id=7
    )
    CONNECT BY prior id=parent_id
  );
```

This uses full table scan and it takes **10 min** to return the data,
However if you use normal sub query or direct values in the "IN" clause it will work fast.

So what is the solution to get the result on the same query with some refactoring?

Approach 2: Using "UNION" method

Just use "UNION" instead of "OR" clause as below:

```
SELECT * FROM tabl WHERE id=6
UNION
SELECT *
FROM tabl
WHERE id IN
  (SELECT id
  FROM tabl
    START WITH parent_id IN
    (SELECT id FROM tabl WHERE id=7
    )
    CONNECT BY prior id=parent_id
  );
```

This uses index scan and finishes in 5 sec.

The reason behind the performance improvement is because "UNION" just combine two simple operations and hence quick However "OR" clause confuses the optimizer and force it to use sub-optimal explain plan.

Advice 48: Resolve Mutating trigger by "Collection" OR "Global temporary table"

A trigger select from a table which is undergoing change results in an error. Here we will discuss different approaches to resolve this.

Mutation means changing. When a table is undergoing changes and a row level trigger tries to select from or modify that table, then oracle throws mutating table error (ORA-4091).

So when the table is getting modified and subsequently the trigger is fired and the trigger body uses SELECT or any DML on the triggering table, then the trigger will not get the correct value. So mutating error is issued to maintain the data integrity.

Example
One Organization has equipment storage system. In that organization so far only new equipment comes to the repository. However a new need arises: As per the agreement some of the existing equipment may be replaced with some better equipment based on terms and condition.

Requirement is: System should check if the equipment code (OPTCODE+NOMBLOC) is present in the table or not. If it is not present then insert the full details of equipment , If the equipment code is present then remove the existing details of the equipment and insert only the new details with same equipment code (OPTCODE+NOMBLOC)

To resolve this you need to use a trigger, but if we use normal trigger to check if the code being inserted into table is already present in the table then you will get mutating trigger ORA-04091 error.
You can remove the mutating trigger error by using autonomous transaction. However if you make the trigger autonomous then the trigger cannot see the changes done by the insert statement and hence business validation fails and we will get erroneous data (**but no error!**).

There are 2 ways to resolve this:

Approach 1: Using "Collection" method

This solution is to use one package inside which you will store the details fetched by the row level trigger. Then in a statement level trigger you will loop through each record of the table and match against the details inserted by the insert statement and stored in package collection variable. Here is the full code (modified to show the lighter version)

```
CREATE TABLE COMP_INVENTORY_T
  ( OPTCODE NUMBER(10), NOMBLOC VARCHAR2(100)
  );


CREATE OR REPLACE
PACKAGE pack_1
AS
Type rec IS TABLE OF COMP_INVENTORY_T%ROWTYPE INDEX BY binary_integer;
  L_inv_rec rec;
END;
/

CREATE OR REPLACE TRIGGER mutate_row_level_trig Before
  INSERT ON COMP_INVENTORY_T FOR EACH row
  DECLARE
  I NUMBER :=pack_1.L_inv_rec.count+1;
  BEGIN
    pack_1.L_inv_rec(i).OPTCODE :=:new.OPTCODE;
    pack_1.L_inv_rec(i).NOMBLOC :=:new.NOMBLOC;
  END;
  /
```

```
CREATE OR REPLACE TRIGGER mutate_statement_level_trig AFTER
  INSERT ON COMP_INVENTORY_T DECLARE X NUMBER;
  v_count NUMBER;
  -- PRAGMA AUTONOMOUS_TRANSACTION;
  BEGIN
    FOR I IN 1..pack_1.L_inv_rec.count
    LOOP
      IF(pack_1.L_inv_rec(i).NOMBLOC = 'OPTION REMISE')
        THEN
        SELECT COUNT(*)
        INTO v_count
        FROM COMP_INVENTORY_T
        WHERE OPTCODE= pack_1.L_inv_rec(i).OPTCODE
        AND NOMBLOC IN ('OPTION INCLUSE','OPTION SOUSCRITE') ;
        dbms_output.put_line('v_count value is:'||v_count);
        IF ( v_count = 0 ) THEN
          NULL;
        END IF ;
        IF ( v_count > 0 ) THEN
          DELETE
          FROM COMP_INVENTORY_T
          WHERE OPTCODE= pack_1.L_inv_rec(i).OPTCODE
          AND NOMBLOC =pack_1.L_inv_rec(i).NOMBLOC;
        END IF ;
      END IF;
    END LOOP;
  END;
  /
```

Approach 2: Using "Global temporary table" method

Alternatively you can use Global temporary table to resolve the nuisance of mutating table

```
CREATE GLOBAL TEMPORARY TABLE inventory_temp_t(
  OPTCODE        NUMBER(10),
  NOMBLOC   VARCHAR2(10)
) ON COMMIT DELETE ROWS;

CREATE OR REPLACE TRIGGER mutate_row_level_trig Before
  INSERT ON COMP_INVENTORY_T FOR EACH row BEGIN
  INSERT
  INTO inventory_temp_t
    (
      OPTCODE,
      NOMBLOC
    )
    VALUES
    (
      :new.OPTCODE,
      :new.NOMBLOC
    );
  END;
error.    /
```

96

```
CREATE OR REPLACE TRIGGER mutate_statement_level_trig AFTER
  INSERT ON COMP_INVENTORY_T DECLARE X NUMBER;
  v_count NUMBER;
  -- PRAGMA AUTONOMOUS_TRANSACTION;
  BEGIN
    FOR I IN
    (SELECT * FROM inventory_temp_t)
    LOOP
      IF(I.NOMBLOC = 'OPTION REMISE') THEN
        SELECT COUNT(*)
        INTO v_count
        FROM COMP_INVENTORY_T
        WHERE OPTCODE= I.OPTCODE
        AND NOMBLOC IN ('OPTION INCLUSE','OPTION SOUSCRITE') ;
        dbms_output.put_line('v_count value is:'||v_count);
        IF ( v_count = 0 ) THEN
          NULL;
        END IF ;
        IF ( v_count > 0 ) THEN
          DELETE FROM COMP_INVENTORY_T
          WHERE OPTCODE= I.OPTCODE AND NOMBLOC =I.NOMBLOC;
        END IF ;
      END IF;
    END LOOP;
  END;
/
```

Using one of these approaches you can resolve mutating table error. However the Global temporary table approach (solution 2) seems to be better solution than PL/SQL collection (solution 1) as when you rollback any DML then the PL/SQL table contents will not be cleaned up.

Advice 49: Auto populate primary key using "TRIGGER" OR "Default value"

Here we will discuss mechanism to auto populate primary key column using sequence without the use of trigger.

Approach 1: Using "TRIGGER" method

Prior to Oracle 12c you cannot use sequence_name.nextval to create a default column value. In order to do that you need to make use of a trigger.

```
CREATE SEQUENCE t_seq START WITH 1;
DROP TABLE t;
CREATE TABLE t
  (a NUMBER PRIMARY KEY,
   b NUMBER DEFAULT 12
  );
CREATE OR REPLACE TRIGGER t_trig BEFORE INSERT ON t FOR EACH ROW
BEGIN
  IF :new.a IS NULL THEN :new.a :=t_seq.nextval;
END IF;
END t_trig;
/
```

Now if you run
```
INSERT INTO t(b) VALUES(24);
```
Table "t" will have a record as below where column A has been populated by the trigger:

A	B
1	1	24

Approach 2: Using "DEFAULT VALUE" method

From Oracle 12c onward you need not use a trigger as you can directly use **nextval** attribute of sequence to create default column value as shown below:

```
CREATE SEQUENCE t_seq START WITH 1;
DROP TABLE t;
CREATE TABLE t
  (a NUMBER DEFAULT t_seq.nextval PRIMARY KEY,
   b NUMBER DEFAULT ON NULL 12
  );
```

Now if you insert a record it will populate the primary key "a" from the sequence t_seq

```
SET serveroutput ON
DECLARE
  var_a NUMBER;
BEGIN
  INSERT INTO t(b) VALUES(17) RETURNING a INTO var_a;
  dbms_output.put_line('value is:'||var_a);
END;
/
```

Output:
```
PL/SQL procedure successfully completed.

value is:1
```

Note: Throughput of application improve dramatically when you use sequence.nextval instead of trigger based approach to populate a default column in 12c.

Here we will discuss number of occurrences of a substring inside a string with and without regular expression.

Approach 1: Using "PL/SQL programming" method

Prior to 11g to get the number of occurrences of a substring in main string you need to develop a user defined function as below

```
CREATE OR REPLACE
FUNCTION f_Count_occurrences(
    p_string    IN CLOB,
    p_substring IN VARCHAR2)
  RETURN NUMBER
IS
  l_occurrences NUMBER;
BEGIN
  IF ( p_string   IS NOT NULL AND p_substring IS NOT NULL ) THEN
    l_occurrences := ( LENGTH(p_string) - ( NVL(LENGTH(REPLACE(p_string,
    p_substring)), 0) ) ) / LENGTH(p_substring) ;
  END IF;
  RETURN ( l_occurrences );
END f_count_occurrences;
/
```

Now when you run
```
SELECT f_Count_occurrences('This is the test for the code', 'the') from dual;
```
You will get output as **2**

Approach 2: Using "PL/SQL programming" method

However in 11g oracle has introduced new regular expression function REGEXP_COUNT. This function will return the number of occurrences of a substring in a string.
When you run:
```
SELECT REGEXP_COUNT('This is the test for the code', 'the') from dual;
```
You will get output as **2**

Ever wondered which query is better, your own query OR parser re-written SQL query of yours.

Approach 1: Using your own query

You need to further tune your query by means of refactoring based on execution plan and probably need to re-write.

Approach 2: Using parser generated query

In Oracle 12c **DBMS_UTILITY.expand_sql_text** provides how oracle parser rewrite the code while doing the expansion of SQL.

E.g.

Let us take the same example to show how oracle rewrite the code internally:

```
SELECT * FROM emp ORDER BY SAL DESC
FETCH NEXT 5 ROWS ONLY;
```

You pass this SQL statement to the **expand_sql_text** as below:

```
SET serveroutput ON
DECLARE
  v_output CLOB;
BEGIN
  DBMS_UTILITY.expand_sql_text( input_sql_text => 'select * from emp order by sal desc fetch next 5 rows only', output_sql_text=>v_output);
  DBMS_OUTPUT.put_line(v_output);
END;
/
```

The <u>output</u> will expand the SQL and shown below how your SQL has been rewritten by oracle parser:

```
SELECT "A1"."EMPLOYEE_ID" "EMPLOYEE_ID",
  "A1"."EMPLOYEE_NAME" "EMPLOYEE_NAME",
  "A1"."JOB" "JOB",
  "A1"."MANAGER_ID" "MANAGER_ID",
  "A1"."HIREDATE" "HIREDATE",
  "A1"."SAL" "SAL",
  "A1"."COMMISSION" "COMMISSION",
  "A1"."DEPARTMENT_ID" "DEPARTMENT_ID"
FROM
  (SELECT "A2"."EMPLOYEE_ID" "EMPLOYEE_ID",
    "A2"."EMPLOYEE_NAME" "EMPLOYEE_NAME",
    "A2"."JOB" "JOB",
    "A2"."MANAGER_ID" "MANAGER_ID",
    "A2"."HIREDATE" "HIREDATE",
    "A2"."SAL" "SAL",
    "A2"."COMMISSION" "COMMISSION",
    "A2"."DEPARTMENT_ID" "DEPARTMENT_ID",
    "A2"."SAL" "rowlimit_$_0",
    ROW_NUMBER() OVER ( ORDER BY "A2"."SAL" DESC ) "rowlimit_$$_rownumber"
  FROM "EMP" "A2"
  ) "A1"
WHERE "A1"."rowlimit_$$_rownumber"<=5
ORDER BY "A1"."rowlimit_$_0" DESC;
```

Now you have a choice between the two queries.

Advice 52: Get distinct count using "COUNT" *OR* "Approx_count_distinct"

Approach 1: Using COUNT function

Count (distinct column name) returns the count of an expression but when the expression evaluates to NULL then that particular record is **not included** in the total.
However this takes some amount of time

Approach 2: Using APPROX_COUNT_DISTINCT function

This function is introduced in oracle 12c.This will give **approximate** total number of **distinct, NOT NULL values of column_name** in a table. Performance improvement using this function is significant as compared to **Count** (distinct column name) and hence when you do not have requirement to display the exact distinct count then you can make use of this function for any of your reporting requirements.

Advice 53: Oracle SQL with "fully qualified column reference" *OR* "No reference"

Here we will discuss how to make Oracle do less work by associating the column with a table alias.

Approach 1: Using "NO REFERENCE"

Generally we need not prefix the table alias against a column if it is present in only single table. However if it is present in more than 1 table it is must to prefix the table alias against the column otherwise it will fail with oracle error (duplicate column found).
But by referencing table alias against each column (no matter if the column is unique or not) you are instructing oracle not to search for each column in each table mentioned in the FROM clause.

e.g.
```
SELECT col1,col2,col3 FROM tab1 a,tab2 b,tab3 c WHERE a.id=b.id AND b.id=c.id;
```

This example does not fully qualify the column references and hence Oracle needs to search for the existence of col1, col2, col3 in all 3 tables.

Approach 2: Using "Fully Qualified Column REFERENCE"

When you are joining multiple tables and selecting certain columns you must make sure you specify the column by prefixing the table or table alias. If we do not specify the table alias against the column Oracle will search each table in the "from" clause to find out the actual table from which the column is present.
Generally we need not prefix the table alias against a column if it is present in only single table. However if it is present in more than 1 table it is must to prefix the table alias against the column otherwise it will fail with oracle error (duplicate column found).
But by referencing table alias against each column (no matter if the column is unique or not) you are instructing oracle not to search for each column in each table mentioned in the FROM clause.

e.g.
```
SELECT col1,col2,col3 FROM tab1 a,tab2 b,tab3 c WHERE a.id=b.id AND b.id=c.id;
```

This example does not fully qualify the column references and hence Oracle needs to search for the existence of col1, col2, col3 in all 3 tables.

In order to fully qualify the column reference here is the code

```
SELECT a.coll,
  b.col2,
  c.col3
FROM tab1 a,
  tab2 b,
  tab3 c
WHERE a.id=b.id
AND b.id  =c.id;
```

So in a nutshell importance of aliases from performance point of view:

- Reduce parse time as oracle engine will not check all the tables and their columns listed in the FROM clause, It will check only the specific table corresponding to the aliased table/column.

- Prevent syntax error occurring when ambiguous column names are added.
  For example

```
SELECT a.empno,
  tax_no,
  b.company_code
FROM emp a,
  company b
WHERE a.comp_code=b.company_code;
```

  Now suppose "tax_no" column is added to table COMPANY then the above query will fail.
  However if we aliased the above query by using a.tax_no then you will never encounter the error.

- Aliases make the query more compact and easy to debug and maintain.

Advice 54: Delete *OR* Truncate

Want to remove data from table? There are 2 ways to do this.

Approach 1: Using "DELETE"

In this approach you can roll back the transaction. You can partially delete some part of the table.
Only problem with this approach is that when you delete the high water mark is not reset.
High water mark is the space used by object. By resetting high water mark to zero we de-allocate all the space and let other object/transactions use the space. This is not possible using delete.

The table with high water mark set to high value, not only occupy huge space which cannot be used by oracle but this issue affect the performance of application because now oracle has to do full table scan of the table with more number of blocks (**more than the actual number of blocks because of unused blocks**) to get the required data.

Here is one example to display how "DELETE" operation create unused space and "TRUNCATE" de-allocate the unused space. The solution to reclaim space if you use "DELETE"

```
CREATE TABLE t2 AS
SELECT * FROM all_objects;
```

This has 1 million records.

Note: [Without collecting statistics if you would like to know the high water mark (size in blocks occupied by a table) use:

```
SELECT COUNT(DISTINCT dbms_rowid.rowid_block_number(rowid)) no_of_blocks
FROM t2;
```

Collect statistics:

```
ANALYZE TABLE T2 compute statistics;
```

Now see the **actual size of table** and **high_water_mark_in_bytes** (**projected size of the table**).
Note the column "**BLOCKS**" signify the high water mark i.e. the projected size of table.
8192 is the size of each BLOCKS (in bytes) in your database.

```
SELECT table_name,
   AVG_ROW_LEN*NUM_ROWS actual_size_in_bytes,
   blocks     *8192 high_water_mark_in_bytes
FROM dba_tables
WHERE owner   ='SCHEMA_NAME'
AND table_name='T2';
```

You can see the high water mark is not reset and hence projected size is much bigger than actual size.

Solution to reclaim space if there is DELETE:

In order to reclaim the unused space here are the steps:

```
ALTER TABLE t2 enable row movement;

ALTER TABLE t2 shrink space;

ANALYZE TABLE t2 compute statistics;
```

Note: If the table has flashback enabled then you must first disable flashback and then shrink the space.

You can shrink the space associated with any index segments also using the CASCADE clause:

```
ALTER TABLE t2 shrink space CASCADE;
```


Approach 2: Using "TRUNCATE"

Advantage:
1. It does the auto commit as it is DDL command
2. It reset the high water mark for the table. **High water mark** is the space used by object. By resetting high water mark to zero we de-allocate all the space and let other object/transactions use the space. This is not possible using delete.
3. It is very fast as compared to delete.

Disadvantage:
1. You cannot rollback the transaction.
2. If the parent table has got the primary key which is referred to by child table then you cannot truncate the table even if the child table does not have any records.
3. You cannot truncate part of the data. You have to either delete all data or none. However if the table is partitioned then you can truncate a single partition instead of whole table.

Now if you use "TRUNCATE" the projected size is showing correctly as high water mark (**blocks**) is reset.

Here is one example to display how "TRUNCATE" operation de-allocate the unused space.

```
TRUNCATE TABLE T2;
ANALYZE TABLE T2 compute statistics;
```

Now see the **actual size of table** and **high_water_mark_in_bytes** (**projected size of the table**) after the truncate operation.

```
SELECT table_name,
  AVG_ROW_LEN*NUM_ROWS actual_size_in_bytes,
  blocks     *8192 high_water_mark_in_bytes
FROM dba_tables
WHERE owner   ='SCHEMA_NAME'
AND table_name='T2';
```

You can see the high water mark is reset and hence projected size and actual size are almost same.

Advice 55: Single column LOOKUP *OR* MULTI column LOOKUP

Here we will discuss how to reduce table I/O by refactoring a query. There are 2 approaches.

I/O is the most important component of response time because oracle has to access the data block from the physical disk. By means of re-sequencing/reorganizing table data you can reduce the disk I/O to a large extent.
There is another way to reduce the disk I/O by means of reducing the number of table lookups. By minimizing the table lookups you can reduce the physical data block access and hence improve the response time of database operation for "select" or "update" as shown below.

Approach 1: SINGLE column LOOKUP

```
  SELECT *
FROM some_table
WHERE column1 IN
  (SELECT column1 FROM tab1
  )
AND column2 IN
  (SELECT column2 FROM tab1
  );


UPDATE some_table set column1= (SELECT column1 FROM tab1 where val=12)
, column2 =(SELECT column2 FROM tab1 where val=12)
WHERE id=3001;
```

You can see we are using lookup for a single column individually which will incur more disk I/O as you are having more number of table lookup.

Approach 2: MULTI column LOOKUP

```
SELECT *
FROM some_table
WHERE (column1,column2) IN
  (SELECT column1,column2 FROM tab1
  );


UPDATE some_table set (column1,column2)
= (SELECT column1,column2 FROM tab1 where val=12)
WHERE id=3001;
```

You can see we are using lookup for a 2 column with a single table lookup.
This will reduce the disk I/O to a large extent.

Advice 56: Sensitive data masking using REDACTION *OR* FGAC (DBMS_RLS)

Here we will discuss how to anonymize or mask sensitive data in 12c and prior to 12c in order to protect data from unwanted exposure.

Prior to 12c you could anonymize or mask sensitive data using FGAC/VPD or by using procedural approach of masking data by implementing some rules and then de-masking the data using the reverse rule. However in 12c using data redaction policy you can on the fly mask any sensitive data of a table. Oracle 12c Redaction is the extension to the FGAC/VPD used for masking in 10g.
Oracle Data Masking is available only with Enterprise Edition and it requires licensing of Advanced Security.

Approach 1: Using FGAC (DBMS_RLS) approach

Prior to 12c (in 10g) solution:

Connect to sys:

```
GRANT EXECUTE ON dbms_rls TO U1;
```
Connect to U1:

```
create table dc_cust(ID number,bank_acc number(10),bank_name varchar2(30));

insert into dc_cust values(1,1234567898,'ABC bank');
insert into dc_cust values(2,1234566897,'ABC bank');
insert into dc_cust values(3,1234565896,'ABC bank');
insert into dc_cust values(4,1234564895,'ABC bank');
insert into dc_cust values(5,1234563894,'ABC bank');
insert into dc_cust values(6,1234562893,'ABC bank');
commit;


CREATE OR REPLACE FUNCTION dc_bank_f (v_owner IN VARCHAR2, v_tab IN VARCHAR2)
RETURN VARCHAR2 AS
  v_rule VARCHAR2 (200);
BEGIN
  v_rule := 'id >0';
  RETURN (v_rule);
END dc_bank_f;
/
```

This function set the rule as to which records the masking will be implemented
So if you give ID between 10 and 30 then the masking of bank_acc will happen only
for those ID, Other ID will have full bank_acc displayed.

```
BEGIN
  DBMS_RLS.ADD_POLICY (object_schema      => 'U1',
                       object_name        => 'dc_cust',
                       policy_name        => 'mask_bank_acc',
                       function_schema    => 'U1',
                       policy_function    => 'dc_bank_f',
                       sec_relevant_cols  => 'bank_acc',
                       sec_relevant_cols_opt => DBMS_RLS.ALL_ROWS);
END;
/
```

Name of the table on which you will mask the sensitive columns

This will state list of columns
(separated by commas) will be masked

This allows to display all the row of the table
But mask only the value as per function dc_bank_f

Now when you run

```
select id,bank_acc,bank_name from dc_cust;
```

The bank_acc value will be masked:

ID	BANK_ACC	BANK_NAME
1		ABC bank
2		ABC bank
3		ABC bank
4		ABC bank
5		ABC bank
6		ABC bank

In order to de-mask or remove the masking use this:

```
BEGIN
  DBMS_RLS.DROP_POLICY (object_schema  => 'U1',
                        object_name    => 'dc_cust',
                        policy_name    => 'mask_bank_acc');
END;
/
```

Approach 2: Using REDACTION approach

Oracle 12c (and also backported to 11.2.0.4) has introduced DBMS_REDACT package to define redaction policy for masking sensitive data of tables and this provides greater level of control and protection of sensitive data and it is much easier to implement as shown below:

Data redaction is part of advanced security option. It does not change the actual data, it just hides the sensitive data from the unauthorized user.

12c solution for full masking:

Connect to sys:

```
GRANT EXECUTE ON sys.dbms_redact TO U1;
```

Connect to U1:

```
BEGIN
  DBMS_REDACT.add_policy(
    object_schema => 'U1',
    object_name   => 'dc_cust',
    column_name   => 'bank_acc',        This will state list of columns
                                        (separated by commas) will be masked
    policy_name   => 'redact_mask_bank_acc',
    function_type => DBMS_REDACT.full,  Function_type state what kind of masking will take
                                        Place like if it is full or some part of the string of the
    expression    => '1=1'              sensitive column will be masked
  );
END;
/                This means redaction will always take place
```

Expression=>'1=1' means masking will happen for all users. However if you want to implement the masking for a set of users or not to mask for a set of users then use the following expression instead of "1=1"

```
expression      => 'SYS_CONTEXT(''USERENV'',''SESSION_USER'') != ''U2'''
```

This means redaction/masking will not take place for schema "U2" and hence from schema u2 if you run "select * from U1.dc_cust;" you will see actually original value (not the masked value of bank_acc.

Now when you run from user U1

```
select id,bank_acc,bank_name from dc_cust;
```

You will get bank_acc value masked to 0:

ID	BANK_ACC	BANK_NAME
1	0	ABC bank
2	0	ABC bank
3	0	ABC bank
4	0	ABC bank
5	0	ABC bank
6	0	ABC bank

12c solution for using substituted value:

If you want to display the substituted value instead of original value you can do that by adding additional parameter [FUNCTION_PARAMETRS] in add_policy or alter_policy function as shown below:

```
BEGIN
  DBMS_REDACT.alter_policy (
    object_schema      => 'U1',
    object_name        => 'dc_cust',
    policy_name        => 'redact_mask_bank_acc',
    action             => DBMS_REDACT.modify_column,
    column_name        => 'bank_acc',
    function_type      => DBMS_REDACT.partial, <——  Function_type state what kind of masking will take
    function_parameters => '9,1,6'                   Place like if it is partial then some part of the string of the
  );                                                 sensitive column will be masked as per function_parameters
END;
/
```

This state how the redaction will be masked.
1st parameter 9: value to be masked to
2nd parameter 1: start point of the string to be masked
3rd parameter 6: end point of the string to be masked

So here 1st to 6th character of bank_acc column value will be replaced by 9

If the data type of **column** (Intended to be masked) is other than **number** then function_parameters will accordingly use different type of values/arguments.

Now when you run
```
select id,bank_acc,bank_name from dc_cust;
```
You will get bank_acc 1 to 6th character values masked to 9:

ID	BANK_ACC	BANK_NAME
1	9999997898	ABC bank
2	9999996897	ABC bank
3	9999995896	ABC bank
4	9999994895	ABC bank
5	9999993894	ABC bank
6	9999992893	ABC bank

From SQLDEVELOPER you can do this by selecting Add Redaction policy and subsequently adding a policy function.

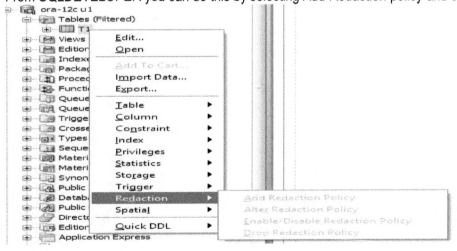

In order to de-mask (disable redaction) or remove the masking use this in oracle 12c:

```
BEGIN
  DBMS_REDACT.drop_policy (
    object_schema => 'U1',
    object_name   => 'dc_cust',
    policy_name   => 'redact_mask_bank_acc'
  );
END;
/
```

Note: Redaction policy is not applicable for Sys user because SYS has "EXEMPT REDACTION POLICY" and hence if you run the following from SYS user:

`SELECT id,bank_acc,bank_name FROM ul.dc_cust;`

It will show bank_acc without any kind of masking.

Advice 57: Sequence fetching using "An expression" *OR* "Queries"

Prior to 11g **currval** and **nextval** attribute of a sequence can be accessed in PL/SQL through queries only.
Oracle 11g has introduced sequence fetching as an expression in a PL/SQL block which is easy to read and maintain.

Approach 1: Using SELECT QUERIES approach

Prior to 11g solution
```
declare
a number;
begin
select test_seq.nextval into a from dual;
end;
/
```
This runs successfully prior to and in 11g.

Approach 2: Using "AN EXPRESSION" approach

11g solution
```
declare
a number;
begin
a :=test_seq.nextval;
end;
/
```
If you run this prior to 11g it will fail, but in 11g it works fine.

Note: NEXTVAL and CURRVAL cannot be used in query/view as column in SELECT statement with DISTINCT, INTERSECT, UNION, MINUS, ORDER BY, GROUP BY and HAVING clause.

So the solution is: First **form an inline view** using the above clauses and then select from the inline view and add the attribute seq_name.nextval in the query as below:

```
SELECT seq_name.nextval,
       a,
       b
FROM
     (SELECT DISTINCT a,b FROM table_name ORDER BY 1
     );
```

Advice 58: PL/SQL compilation in "INTERPRETED MODE" *OR* "NATIVE MODE"

Here we will see how to compile a code using interpreted mode and native mode.

Approach 1: PL/SQL compilation in "INTERPRETED MODE" approach

PL/SQL default compilation compiles the PL/SQL code as interpreted 'P-Code' and <u>stored</u> in system tablespace of the database.

Approach 2: PL/SQL compilation in "NATIVE MODE" approach

PL/SQL Native compilation compiles the PL/SQL code as native code instead of interpreted 'P-Code' and <u>stored</u> in system tablespace of the database.
Prior to 11g, the PL/SQL native compiler translated the PL/SQL code into C code and then external C compiler translated the C code into the native code. So in a nutshell you need to have the following to compile PL/SQL code <u>natively prior to oracle 11g</u>.
  ➢ C compiler in the server
  ➢ PLSQL_NATIVE_LIBRARY_DIR parameter must be set and point to the os directory
  ➢ PLSQL_CODE_TYPE needs to be set to 'NATIVE'

However in 11g PL/SQL native compiler can generate native code directly.
You need to just do this, so simple:
  ➢ PLSQL_CODE_TYPE needs to be set to 'NATIVE'

Example how it works in 11g:
```
create or replace procedure native_test_proc
is
BEGIN
  FOR i IN 1 .. 6
  LOOP
    IF i IN (3,5) THEN
      CONTINUE;
    END IF;
    DBMS_OUTPUT.PUT_LINE('current ieration is: ' || TO_CHAR(i));
  END LOOP;
END native_test_proc;
/
```
In order to natively compile this normal PL/SQL code do this:
```
ALTER PROCEDURE native_test_proc COMPILE PLSQL_CODE_TYPE = NATIVE;
```
You can control the setting in session and system level:

For session level:

```
ALTER session SET PLSQL_CODE_TYPE='NATIVE';
ALTER PROCEDURE native_test_proc COMPILE;
```
For system level:
```
ALTER SYSTEM SET PLSQL_CODE_TYPE='NATIVE';
ALTER PROCEDURE native_test_proc COMPILE;
```

You can see the setting using this:
```
SELECT name, type, plsql_code_type
    FROM  user_plsql_object_settings
    WHERE  name = 'NATIVE_TEST_PROC';
```
Output:

NAME	TYPE	PLSQL_CODE_TYPE
NATIVE_TEST_PROC	PROCEDURE	NATIVE

In order to set it to interpreted level just do this:
```
ALTER PROCEDURE native_test_proc COMPILE PLSQL_CODE_TYPE = INTERPRETED;
```

When you have computation intensive code in your PL/SQL code then it is advisable to compile NATIVELY, using just 1 liner setup to set it to 'NATIVE', as this will give significant performance enhancement. However if you compile code (default mode INTERPRETED) normally then the code is stored in an intermediate form and needs to be interpreted at runtime and hence performs slower than NATIVELY compiled code.

Advice 59: Use "BIND VARIABLE" OR "NO BIND VARIABLE"

Here we will discuss how to parse a code once and execute multiple times to improve performance.

When dynamically we want to process each record from any table then we must design the code to have "one parse and multiple executes" instead of "multiple parse and multiple executes".
Performance improves from 5 hours to 10 minutes by using this strategy when we have more than 90000 records in 1 table.
In this example all the tables are queried dynamically based on their primary key (which are also formed dynamically).

Approach 1: "NO BIND VARIABLE" approach

See the code snippets

111

```
BEGIN
--This will get SCN number for the date from which we would like to process data
SELECT Timestamp_to_scn(sync_from_date) INTO fr_scn FROM dual;
--This will get SCN number for the date to which we would like to process data
SELECT Timestamp_to_scn(sync_to_date) INTO to_scn FROM dual;
--This LOOP contains list of table to be migrated
FOR i IN (SELECT table_name FROM MAPPING_TABLE) LOOP

    --This is the LOOP which get primary key column for a table
    FOR m_data IN (SELECT column_position, ai.column_name
      FROM all_ind_columns ai, all_constraints ac
      WHERE ai.table_name    =ac.table_name
      AND ai.table_name      =i.table_name
      AND ai.table_owner     ='user_nm'
      AND ac.owner           = 'user_nm'
      AND ac.constraint_type ='P'
      AND ac.constraint_name =ai.index_name  order by 1) LOOP

        IF m_data.column_position =1 THEN
          sel_stmt   :='select '||m_data.column_name||' as pkey_value1';
          pkey_name1 :=m_data.column_name;
          pkey_count :=1;
        elsif m_data.column_position=2 THEN
          sel_stmt   :=sel_stmt||','|| m_data.column_name||' as pkey_value2';
          pkey_name2  :=m_data.column_name;
          pkey_count  :=2;
        elsif m_data.column_position=3 THEN
          --as above(here the table contain primary key with three columns)
        END IF;
    END LOOP; --This is the END LOOP which derived all the primary key column for a table
--This below sel_stmt will form the select statement to extract the version date between 2 scn numbers
sel_stmt :=sel_stmt||',versions_starttime,versions_startscn,versions_operation from '||'user_nm'||i.table_name||' '||'VERSIONS
BETWEEN SCN '||fr_scn ||' and '|| to_scn ||' WHERE VERSIONS_OPERATION is NOT NULL AND versions_startscn>='||fr_scn ||' AND versions_startscn<'||
to_scn ||' order by versions_startscn,versions_operation';
--This will bulk collect primary key value, version starttime and version operation for a table.
EXECUTE immediate sel_stmt bulk collect INTO v_pkey_1_idx_tab,v_ver_starttime_tab,v_ver_startscn_tab,v_ver_operation_tab;

  FOR each_tab_rec IN 1..v_pkey_1_idx_tab.count LOOP --This will update,delete each records in a table between 2 SCNs
    IF v_ver_operation_tab(each_tab_rec) ='U' THEN
      EXECUTE immediate 'update '||i.table_name||' set m_END_DATE=v_ver_starttime_tab(each_tab_rec)'||',m_UPDATE_DATE=systimestamp where '||
      pkey_name1||'=v_pkey_1_idx_tab(each_tab_rec)'||' and m_END_DATE is NULL
      and m_DELETE_DATE is NULL AND m_START_DATE <v_ver_starttime_tab(each_tab_rec)';
    END IF;
  END LOOP;--End loop for update and delete of records in a table between 2 SCNs
END LOOP;   --end of main loop which works for each table present in MAPPING_TABLE
END;
/
```

Do you find any issue in the above code?
If you closely observe you can see the dynamic query is formed for each record of each table. So if in 1 table you have 1 million records then the dynamic query shown will be formed 1 million times and will kill the performance.

Approach 2: "BIND VARIABLE" approach

The way out is to form the dynamic query for each table for only one time and execute the query using bind variables provided through USING clause.

Note that you cannot use bind variables in your dynamic query for Oracle identifiers (e.g. Table name and column name [**pkey_name**1]) and hence we used normal variable to form the query and not bind it by bind variable.

```
DECLARE
--declare all variables......
BEGIN
--This will get SCN number for the date from which we would like to process data
SELECT Timestamp_to_scn(sync_from_date) INTO fr_scn FROM dual;
--This will get SCN number for the date to which we would like to process data
SELECT Timestamp_to_scn(sync_to_date) INTO to_scn FROM dual;
--This LOOP contains list of table to be migrated
FOR i IN (SELECT table_name FROM MAPPING_TABLE) LOOP

   --This is the LOOP which get primary key column for a table
   FOR m_data IN (SELECT column_position, ai.column_name
     FROM all_ind_columns ai, all_constraints ac
     WHERE ai.table_name    =ac.table_name
     AND ai.table_name      =i.table_name
     AND ai.table_owner     = 'user_nm'
     AND ac.owner           = 'user_nm'
     AND ac.constraint_type ='P'
     AND ac.constraint_name =ai.index_name   order by 1) LOOP

     IF m_data.column_position =1 THEN
        sel_stmt   :='select '||m_data.column_name||' as pkey_value1';
        pkey_name1 :=m_data.column_name;
        pkey_count :=1;
     elsif m_data.column_position=2 THEN
        sel_stmt   :=sel_stmt||','|| m_data.column_name||' as pkey_value2';
        pkey_name2 :=m_data.column_name;
        pkey_count :=2;
     elsif m_data.column_position=3 THEN
        --as above(here the table contain primary key with three columns)
        END IF;
     END LOOP; --This is the END LOOP which derived all the primary key column for a table
--This below sel_stmt will form the select statement to extract the version date between 2 scn numbers
sel_stmt :=sel_stmt||',versions_starttime,versions_startscn,versions_operation from '||'user_nm'||i.table_name||' '||'VERSIONS
BETWEEN  SCN '||fr_scn ||' and '||to_scn ||' WHERE VERSIONS_OPERATION is NOT NULL AND versions_startscn>='||fr_scn ||' AND versions_startscn<'||
to_scn ||' order by versions_startscn,versions_operation';
--This will bulk collect primary key value, version starttime and version operation for a table.
EXECUTE immediate sel_stmt bulk collect INTO v_pkey_1_idx_tab,v_ver_starttime_tab,v_ver_startscn_tab,v_ver_operation_tab;
--This will form (only one time for each table)the dynamic update statement with bind variable.
u_update_stmt :='update '||i.table_name||' set m_END_DATE=:1'||',m_UPDATE_DATE=systimestamp where '||pkey_name1||'=:2'||' and m_END_DATE is NULL
   and m_DELETE_DATE is NULL AND m_START_DATE <:3';

   FOR each_tab_rec IN 1..v_pkey_1_idx_tab.count LOOP --This will update,delete each records in a table between 2 SCNs
      IF v_ver_operation_tab(each_tab_rec) ='U' THEN
      EXECUTE immediate u_update_stmt USING v_ver_starttime_tab(each_tab_rec),v_pkey_1_idx_tab(each_tab_rec),v_ver_starttime_tab(each_tab_rec);
      END IF;
   END LOOP;--End loop for update and delete of records in a table between 2 SCNs
END LOOP;   --end of main loop which works for each table present in MAPPING_TABLE
END;
/
```

The difference between two approaches are:

- ➢ Approach 1 was not using **bind variables** whereas approach 2 **uses** them.
- ➢ Approach 1 forms the string for each record inside "FOR each_tab_rec IN 1..." Loop however Approach 2 forms the string only once before the LOOP.
- ➢ Approach 1 undergoes **many parses** and **many executes** whereas Approach 2 uses **one parse many executes** as it uses **bind variables** which result into improved performance. This behaviour is because oracle checks if the exact full statement is there in library cache by calculating hash value of the sql string. So if you do not use bind variable and use literal then each time the hash value of sql string will be different and hence for every **new** hash value of the string there will be hard parse. However if you use bind variable then the hash value of the SQL string is same and hence there will be one parse instead of millions of parse.

Advice 60: BULK OPERATION using "LIMIT" *OR* "NO LIMIT"

Bulk operation process multiple rows at a time and reduce the context switching between SQL and PL/SQL engines. However there are scenario where BULK operation hinder performance. Here we will see how to resolve the use BULK operation without any hindrance to performance.

BULK COLLECT: In a single fetch retrieve multiple rows. SELECT statement uses this clause.
FORALL: Change multiple rows quickly by sending all the DML to SQL engine from PL/SQL engine with just one context switch.

Approach 1: Default BULK OPERATION approach

```
DECLARE
  CURSOR C1 IS SELECT * FROM employee;
  TYPE t1 IS TABLE OF C1%ROWTYPE INDEX BY BINARY_INTEGER;
  v_emp t1;
BEGIN
  OPEN C1;
  LOOP
    FETCH C1 BULK COLLECT INTO v_emp;
    EXIT WHEN v_emp.COUNT=0;
    FORALL i IN 1 .. v_emp.COUNT
    UPDATE employee SET salary =salary*1.5 WHERE emp_id=v_emp(i).emp_id;
  END LOOP;
  CLOSE C1;
END;
/
```

Suppose you fetch millions of rows in a collection variable which will consume a huge amount of memory in PGA for that session and similarly another 100 users also call the same program and consume a huge amount of PGA memory. This will result in performance degradation for other application running in the system because of excessive PGA swapping.

Again via network when you update millions of rows using bulk binding it may cause network slowness because all the rows you bulk fetched into a collection may not be accommodated in the PGA and hence slow down the performance because of excessive swapping which slam the network.

If you fetch a single row at a time it is too slow and takes a long time to process millions of rows so bulk fetch is essential but not at the cost of jamming the network by causing performance degradation across the system.

114

So Bulk operation improve performance however there are scenarios where they will **hinder performance of the system as explained**

Approach 2: BULK OPERATION using "LIMIT" approach

So for effective performance improvement using BULK COLLECT there should be a trade-off between bulk operation and huge PGA memory consumption.

You can control the amount of PGA memory consumption by bulk collect using **"LIMIT"** clause
This way you get the benefit of BULK COLLECT and not allowing the PGA memory swapping to happen.

```
DECLARE
   CURSOR C1 IS SELECT * FROM employee;
   TYPE t1 IS TABLE OF C1%ROWTYPE INDEX BY BINARY_INTEGER;
   v_emp t1;
BEGIN
   OPEN C1;
   LOOP
     FETCH C1 BULK COLLECT INTO v_emp LIMIT 10000;
     EXIT WHEN v_emp.COUNT=0;
     FORALL i IN 1 .. v_emp.COUNT
     UPDATE employee SET salary =salary*1.5 WHERE emp_id=v_emp(i).emp_id;
   END LOOP;
   CLOSE C1;
END;
/
```

So using **"LIMIT"** clause you bulk fetch **10000** rows at a time instead of 1 million rows and hence this consume considerably less amount of PGA memory but process all the rows like a nice steady stream of data.

Advice 61: Find value of bind variable while running an application

Here we will discuss a way to find how far your PL/SQL code has been executed by extracting the value of bind variable at particular point of time.

We have seen it is sometimes important to know how far your code has been executed as it runs.
Currently when a top level query is running, the log will record when each subquery starts and finishes but when a subquery using a bind variable is running, the current value of the bind variable is not shown. In order to know the bind variable value whilst the subquery is running, use the following query:

```
SELECT DISTINCT Sq.Sql_Text,
  Spc.Name,
  SUBSTR(Spc.Value_String,1,15) bind_value
FROM V$Sql_Bind_Capture Spc,
  V$Session S,
  V$Sql Sq
WHERE S.Sql_Hash_Value =Spc.Hash_Value
AND S.Sql_Address       = Spc.Address
AND Sq.Sql_Id           =S.Sql_Id
AND spc.was_captured    ='YES';
```

Advice 62: Adaptive query optimization and online stats gathering in 12c

Here we will discuss improvement in accuracy of execution plan and enhancement in online statistics gathering in 12c.

Adaptive query optimization is the **new feature** in 12c which helps the optimizer to improve the accuracy of an execution plan.

The purpose of oracle optimizer is to determine the best execution plan for a SQL statement. It makes the decision based on the statistics available and the optimizer used and execution features available in the Oracle release.
If no statistics are available then using dynamic sampling it generates some sample statistics and decides the execution plan.
Please note fixed object statistics (pre 12c approach) do not always give sufficient information to find the most accurate and best execution plan.

In Oracle 12c Oracle has introduced **adaptive query optimization**. This consist of **2 aspects**:

Adaptive plan: This enables the optimizer to delay the final execution plan until the execution of the query is completed. This is done by making adjustments at run-time using dynamic sampling and cardinality feedback. As the query runs, information is collected from and passed between each part of the execution plan, allowing the adaptive plan to switch between the HASH and NESTED LOOP join methods as required.

Adaptive statistics: This provides additional information to improve subsequent execution of the query.

Online stats gathering:
In oracle 12c dynamic sampling has been enhanced to have online stats gathering (known as dynamic statistics). The dynamic stats improve the existing statistics by getting more accurate cardinality estimates for tables, Join clause, group clause etc. Initialization parameter OPTIMIZER_DYNAMIC_SAMPLING value "11" enables the optimizer to automatically collect dynamic statistics.
For example, because online stats gathering results are instantly available to the optimizer, we have seen substantial performance improvement when using CTAS (Create table as select * from) and IAS (Insert into ...Select * from).

Note: If optimizer is not using correct execution plan the query which is expected to finish in few minutes might take few hours due to incorrect cardinality estimates, absence of statistics or out of date statistics.

Here we will demonstrate that addition of default nullable column in pre-12c, locks the system for a certain duration and generates huge undo and redo, however in 12c this issue is resolved.

In Oracle 11g if you need to add a default column which can be nullable it takes a significant amount of time. However if the default column is not nullable then it is instantaneous.
So the addition of a nullable default column performance issue is addressed in Oracle 12c

Here is one example
Run this in Oracle 11g:
```
CREATE TABLE t2 AS
SELECT * FROM all_objects;
```

Add a default column which is NOT NULL,
```
ALTER TABLE t2 ADD (c5 CHAR(100) DEFAULT 'yes' NOT NULL)
```
This takes 0.4 sec.

Add a default column which is NULLABLE,
```
ALTER TABLE t2 ADD (c6 CHAR(100) DEFAULT 'yes')
```
This takes 15-25 sec and for this duration it will lock the entire table. Also this operation generates large amount of undo and redo.

However, when you run exactly same operations in **12c** both will take less than 0.4 sec and there is no locking.

To see the size growth of the table you can do as below in 11g and 12c:
Step 1:

```
ANALYZE TABLE T2 compute statistics;

SELECT AVG_ROW_LEN*NUM_ROWS/1024/1024
  ||' MB' size_of_table
FROM all_tables
WHERE owner   ='SCHEMA_NAME'
AND table_name='T2';
```

Step 2:
```
ALTER TABLE t2 ADD (c6 CHAR(100) DEFAULT 'yes')
```
Step 3:
```
ANALYZE TABLE T2 compute statistics;

SELECT AVG_ROW_LEN*NUM_ROWS/1024/1024
  ||' MB' size_of_table
FROM all_tables
WHERE owner   ='SCHEMA_NAME'
AND table_name='T2';
```

117

You can see there is significant growth in table size in oracle 11g, However in oracle 12c the growth is nominal.

Advice 64: Enhance performance by adjusting Oracle clustering Factor

Here we will understand oracle clustering factor and the importance of organizing table data to improve query performance. Clustering factor is a measure of how data in a table is organized and sequenced so that an index scan can retrieve the data with the least effort by searching only a few data blocks instead of all data blocks.
A simple example to visualize this is as below:
You are asked to get 10 rows from a table and these 10 rows are located in 10 different data blocks rather than in a single data block.
A low clustering factor signifies that the data in a table is sequenced with respect to index whereas a high clustering factor signifies that the data in a table is out of sequence with the index and hence an index range scan will consume lots of IO. So lower the clustering factor, the better the table is organized, and higher the clustering factor the more the table data is scattered.

```
SELECT index_name,
  clustering_factor,
  num_rows
FROM dba_indexes
WHERE table_name='<Table name>';
```

This provides information on how the table data is synchronized with the index.
If we have an index with a low clustering factor value then the optimizer will prefer to use an index scan, if we have an index with a high clustering factor value then the optimizer will prefer not to use an index scan and may choose a table scan.

So, as a rule, DBA will need to re-sequence the table rows in situations where, in your application, the majority of SQL refers to a column with high clustering factor value. Please note by reorganizing the table based on the column which is mostly used you can lower the clustering factor of that index column however the clustering factor of other columns will be impacted. So there is a trade-off between performance gain by sequencing rows based on the column which is mostly used and performance penalty by disturbing the clustering factor of the other index columns which are not used widely.
So by reorganizing the table [by means of dbms_redefinition utility or by any other
Means like
-Recreating the table/or reinserting data with ORDER BY clause from temp table
-Recreating the table/or reinserting data using APPEND hint from temp table
The application as a whole performs with the best response time because both index and table become compact as can be seen by running the query:

After reorganizing table you need to collect statistics:
```
EXEC dbms_stats.gather_table_stats(ownname=>'SCHEMA NAME',tabname=>'TABLE_NAME')
```
Now you can see space used by table:
```
SELECT table_name,
  blocks, --amount of storage space of table
  num_rows
FROM all_tables
WHERE table_name='TABLE_NAME';
```

Now you can see space used by index:

```
SELECT index_name,
  leaf_blocks, --amount of storage space of index
  num_rows
FROM all_indexes
WHERE index_name='INDEX_NAME';
```

You can observe reorganization make both the table and index much compact in size which results in better performance.

Advice 65: Forecast performance of Oracle system

Here we will explore forecasting of oracle performance in an oracle system and ways to improve response time.

Here are some basic steps to forecast the oracle system performance.
We need to know some basic concepts like user calls which you see in tkprof report

User calls: It is number of user calls such as login, parse, fetch, or execute

At a certain time to get the user calls we have below query:
```
SELECT name, value FROM v$sysstat WHERE name = 'user calls';
```

To know amount of user calls generated or to get total raw oracle workload data within certain period, we can run the query before and after a certain interval of time as below:

```
SELECT name, value FROM v$sysstat WHERE name = 'user calls';
```
The output is: user calls   5100
Then tell the system to sleep for 500 seconds
Exec sys.dbms_lock.sleep (500);
Run the user query again to get no of user calls
```
SELECT name, value FROM v$sysstat WHERE name = 'user calls';
```

The output: user   calls 9100

So the **arrival rate** of workload is
= (s1-s0)/T = (9100-5100)/500
=4000/500
 =8
To know what the CPU utilization is we need to run the following command from UNIX
 SAR -u 500 1

Linux 2.6.18-164.11.1.e	12/14/2015 04:33:15 PM	CPU	%user	%nice	%system	%iowait	%steal	%idle
04:34:55 PM	all		15.99	0.00	9.01	0.08	0.00	74.5

So the **CPU utilization** = user time + system time
 =15.99+9.01=25%

Now to derive **service time** for each transaction (Considering it is **10 CPU mchine**) the formula is
svc time= (CPU utilization)*(no of CPU)/ (rate of arrival)
 =.25*10/8
 =0.3125 s

So if you increase no of CPU the svc time will reduce

Now to find the **response time** system formula
Response time= (svc time)/ (1- CPU utilization %)
=0.3125/ (1-0.25)
=0.4166

This way we can forecast the performance of any oracle database system and can take appropriate action like adding more CPU or adding faster CPU, increase CPU utilization etc. to have a better response time.

Note: For the R&D I refer the formula given by Mr. Dan to calculate service time and response time to forecast the oracle system performance

Advice 66: Throughput and response time concept

Here we will understand throughput/response time and ways to improve both.

Throughput is the measure of number of transactions per seconds.
Response time is the measure of average elapsed seconds per records retrieved.
When optimizer **goal** is best throughput you set optimizer_mode=all_rows.
When optimizer **goal** is best response time you set optimizer_mode=first_rows

So when you are working on a Decision Support System where you want to improve the performance of reporting application and at the same time need to have best throughput of the application then you check the top disk usage by top 5 query using the following step:

```
SELECT schema,
  sql_text,
  disk_reads,
  ROUND (cpu, 2)
FROM
  (SELECT s.parsing_schema_name schema,
    t.sql_id,
    t.sql_text,
    t.disk_reads,
    t.sorts,
    t.cpu_time / 1000000 cpu,
    t.rows_processed,
    t.elapsed_time
  FROM v$sqlstats t
  JOIN v$sql s
  ON (t.sql_id            = s.sql_id)
  WHERE parsing_schema_name = 'SCOTT'
  ORDER BY disk_reads DESC
  )
WHERE ROWNUM <= 5;
```

So the challenges are
1. Throughput of the DSS needs to be improved
2. Response time of the reporting application needs to be improved

Please note there are many ways to improve the throughput and response time of an application which you will find in this book. However in this Tips, I will throw light on the "direct path loading and compression perspective" of improving throughput and response time.

To improve the throughput:

Set the table's logging attribute to NOLOGGING thus redo generation for direct path operations is minimized (this feature has no effect on regular DML operations).

1. ALTER TABLE table_name NOLOGGING;
2. Use direct path loading
    Here are the few ways to improve this kind of operation
    a. INSERT /*+ APPEND */ INTO table name SELECT (sub query based on source tables joins)
    b. INSERT /*+ APPEND_VALUES */ INTO table_name VALUES (...........);
    c. DROP table table_name;
        CREATE TABLE table_name as select (sub query based on source tables joins)
3. Use parallel loading
    INSERT /*+ PARALLEL (table_name, 6) */ INTO table name SELECT (sub query based on source tables joins)

For the options 2 a), 2 b) and 3 you must make sure the data is committed immediately after executing the direct path insert, otherwise it will not allow you to "SELECT" the record from that table and the subsequent select will fail with oracle error ORA-12838.

The APPEND hints tell the database to find the last block and placed the newly inserted records at the end of the table's physical storage space (datafiles). This step will write the inserted data directly in the datafiles bypassing data block buffer cache.

Please note point 1 and point 2 combined make the DML very fast.

However if you can combine 1, 2 and 3 steps then it will work extremely fast.

Steps 2 and 3 can be combined to take advantage of APPEND and PARALLEL hints together as below:
    a. INSERT /*+ APPEND PARALLEL(table_name,6) */ INTO table name SELECT (sub query based on source tables joins)

Important thing to consider before using PARALLEL processing: It uses more I/O resource and more processing memory and hence you must make sure the system has enough CPUs. The more CPUs you have the higher the degree of parallelism you can employ in your query.

Total number of threads spawned when you set degree of parallelism to 6:
6*2+1=13 processes or threads generated for the parallel operation.
So a 13 CPU machine is required to run the parallel operation.
The degree of parallelism in a parallel query must be set based on how many CPUs are available.

To improve response time:

When you compress data as it is loaded the data will be compacted into fewer database blocks and thus will require less I/O for subsequent reads from the table and result in improved data retrieval performance.

```
CREATE TABLE t1 COMPRESS AS SELECT * FROM t2;
```
This will create a table with compress data and subsequent direct path load will load the data in compress mode.

To compress a table command is:
```
ALTER TABLE t1 compress;
```

To compress the existing data of the table and activate it for future data loads command is
```
ALTER TABLE t1 move compress;
```

Advice 67: Blocking session and blocked session and top running queries

Here we will find the session that is blocked by some other sessions, and the reason for wait. Also will find the top queries based on I/O, run time.

Here are some frequently used queries which help to find out bottleneck of any oracle issue.

Find blocking session and all the blocked sessions:

```
SELECT sess1.username
   || '@'
   || sess1.machine          ┐ ← ─── Blocking session details
   || ' ( SID='              │
   || sess1.sid              │
   || ' ) is blocking '      ┘
   || sess2.username         ┐
   || '@'                    │
   || sess2.machine          ├ ← ─── Blocked session details
   || ' ( SID='              │
   || sess2.sid              ┘
   || ' ) ' AS block_status
FROM v$lock lock1,
   v$session sess1,
   v$lock lock2,
   v$session sess2
WHERE sess1.sid    =lock1.sid
AND sess2.sid      =lock2.sid
AND lock1.BLOCK    =1
AND lock2.request > 0
AND lock1.id1      = lock2.id1
AND lock1.id2      = lock2.id2 ;
```

Find blocked object using v$LOCKED_OBJECT:

```
SELECT l.oracle_username ,
   o.owner,
   o.object_name,
   o.object_type
FROM v$locked_object l,
   dba_objects o
WHERE l.object_id = o.object_id
```

Find top 5 query for max I/O:

```
SELECT sql_text,
  disk_reads
FROM
  (SELECT sql_text,
    buffer_gets,
    disk_reads,
    sorts,
    cpu_time/1000000 cpu,
    rows_processed,
    elapsed_time
  FROM v$sqlstats
  ORDER BY disk_reads DESC
  )
WHERE rownum <= 5;
```

Find top 5 query for max elapsed/runtime:

```
SELECT sql_text,
  elapsed_time
FROM
  (SELECT sql_text,
    buffer_gets,
    disk_reads,
    sorts,
    cpu_time/1000000 cpu,
    rows_processed,
    elapsed_time
  FROM v$sqlstats
  ORDER BY elapsed_time DESC
  )
WHERE rownum <= 5;
```

Get the reason for wait:
```
SELECT username,
  sid,
  event,
  state,
  wait_time,
  seconds_in_wait
FROM v$session
WHERE state    ='WAITING'
AND event NOT IN ('SQL*Net message to client', 'SQL*Net message from client','rdbms ipc message')
AND username   ='SYS';
```

Here we will explore how to find how far your SQL query has been executed and how much time left to finish execution.

We have seen many times that oracle takes a long time to execute a single query or set of queries.
Here are the steps to find out how long a query will take to complete its execution:

First of all run the following query which will give the top queries and corresponding SID, based on latest run.

```
SELECT s.username,
   s.sid,
   s.status,
   t.sql_text
FROM v$sqltext t,
   v$session s
WHERE t.address   = s.sql_address
AND t.hash_value = s.sql_hash_value
AND s.username    = '<provide the user name>'
ORDER BY s.sid,t.piece;
```

The query can be written as below if you do not have access to v$sqltext

```
SELECT a.sid,
   a.serial#,
   b.sql_text
FROM v$session a,
   v$sqlarea b
WHERE a.sql_address=b.address
AND a.username      ='Provide user name'
ORDER BY a.sid;
```

From the output of the above query you can identify the query you want to know the execution time of and note down the corresponding SID.

To find how much more time the query will take to finish its execution run this:

```
SELECT username,
   target,
   sofar blocks_read_sofar,
   totalwork total_blocks_to_read,
   ROUND(time_remaining/60) minutes
FROM v$session_longops
WHERE sofar    <> totalwork
AND username   = '<Provide the user name>'
AND SID        =<provide the sid value FROM earlier step>;
```

Here we will discuss performance related terminology like selectivity, cardinality and histograms.

Cardinality is the measure of unique number of specific value in a table column.
Selectivity is the measure of variety of the column value in relation to total number of rows in that table.
To derive **selectivity** the formula is:

Selectivity of column1= (Cardinality of column1) * 100 / (Number of rows in the table)

So if we have Table EMP which has 10000 records with columns gender, age, emp_id.
The age can be between 20 and 40

The **cardinality** of gender column is: 2 (male or female)
The **selectivity** of gender column is: 2*100/10000=0.02%

The **cardinality** of age column is: 20 (approx.)
The **selectivity** of age column is: 20*100/10000=0.2%

The **cardinality** of emp_id column is: 10000 (as this is primary key)
The **selectivity** of emp_id column is: 10000*100/10000=100%

Query optimizer uses the selectivity of a column to decide if it is worth to use the index or not to find a certain row in a table.

When data in a certain column is not distributed evenly then it is difficult to predict the **cardinality** or **selectivity** of the column.
The **selectivity of query/index** is derived based on (**Number of indexed rows fetched for certain query*100/Total number of rows**) and hence if the data distribution is skewed you cannot use the generic "**selectivity or cardinality**" formula as this will give wrong result. So for this kind of scenario Oracle provides **Histograms** which predict cardinality.

Histogram is a special type of column statistics which provide detail information about data distribution which are skewed/uneven in nature.

A new feature of the dbms_stats package has the ability to look for columns that should have histograms, and then automatically create the histograms.

By using the below steps Oracle will automatically find the columns which have uneven data distribution and create histograms for them. When you use "Method_opt" as "skewonly" as shown below oracle looks for data distribution of each column and creates histograms only for the columns which have uneven data distribution.

Exec dbms_stats.gather_table_stats ('HR','EMPLOYEES', method_opt=> 'for all columns size skewonly');
HR   -> is name of the Schema
EMPLOYEES   -> name of table

To check which tables and which columns have **histogram statistics** just run this:
```
SELECT column_name,table_name,histogram
FROM DBA_TAB_COLUMNS
WHERE table_name='EMPLOYEES';
```

Advice 70: Find SQL in your application without bind variable

Here we will find how to identify the queries in your application which do not use bind variables.

As you know using bind variable will reduce the hard parse substantially and improve performance however there is still lots of SQL used in an application where bind variables are not used.
In order to find and identify these SQLs here is the code:

```
WITH no_bind AS
        (SELECT force_matching_signature,
                COUNT( * )  matche_count,
                MAX(sql_id || child_number) max_sql_child,
                DENSE_RANK() OVER (ORDER BY COUNT( * ) DESC) AS ranking
         FROM v$sql
         WHERE force_matching_signature <> 0
           AND parsing_schema_name = '<SCHEMA_NAME>'
         GROUP BY force_matching_signature
         HAVING COUNT( * ) > 5)
   SELECT sql_id,matche_count, parsing_schema_name, sql_text
     FROM      v$sql JOIN no_bind
       ON (sql_id || child_number = max_sql_child)
   WHERE ranking <= 10
   ORDER BY matche_count DESC;
```

This will provide us with SQL used in an application which does not use bind variables, is present in the cache with different literals and the same sql occurs more than 5 times with different literals.
In cases where bind variables are used then there would have been only one entry in the cache instead of 6 or more entries for each SQL.

This is very useful to find SQLs which will potentially cause performance problems.

Note: If the application is not using bind variables then there will be an increase in hard parsing which cause performance penalty. So it is advisable to modify the application to use bind variables. However when it is not possible to modify the application, you can still avoid hard parse to some extent using the "**CURSOR_SHARING**" parameter as below:

```
ALTER session SET cursor_sharing=force;  --session level
ALTER system SET cursor_sharing=force;   --system level
```

The parameter "FORCE" lets the database replace the literal values by system generated bind variables which in turn improve performance by reducing number of hard parse considerably. There are some implication when you use this setting, so you must be careful before you set the parameter in SYSTEM level.
To get the system statistics related with amount of hard parse and total parse, just use dynamic performance view V$SYSSTAT

```
SELECT * FROM V$SYSSTAT WHERE NAME LIKE 'parse%';
```

The output:

STATISTIC#	NAME	CLASS	VALUE	STAT_ID
622	parse time cpu	64	259008	206905303
623	parse time elapsed	64	868538	1431595225
624	parse count (total)	64	56326820	63887964
625	parse count (hard)	64	704647	143509059
626	parse count (failures)	64	45726	1118776443
627	parse count (describe)	64	1724	469016317

You can see no of hard parse: 704647 out of total parse: 56326820. Percentage of hard parse=704647*100/56326820 %
In case you see percentage of hard parse is more than 5-10% you must take action to reduce the hard parsing by finding all the SQL which does not use bind variable using query given in this tips.

V$SYSSTAT dynamic view is very handy to get amount of **table scan** happening in the system by using the predicate: 'NAME LIKE 'table scan%'' in the above query

Advice 71: SQL TRACE and TKPROF formatting

Here we will show how to set SQL TRACE and generate human readable trace file using TKPROF utility.

To diagnose a performance issue in an application we trace the SQL activity and then using TKPROF utility we can format the trace file into readable format. Here are the steps:

Connect to user "U1" and run the below steps:

Step 1: start tracing
```
ALTER SESSION SET SQL_TRACE=TRUE;
```

Step 2: Run some SQL queries and also execute some procedure from your application which you would like to trace

Step 3: Get the name of generated trace file using below query. Here p.tracefile will give name and location of trace file.
```
SELECT s.sid,
    s.machine,
    s.username,
    s.port,
    s.terminal,
    s.program,
    s.sql_id,
    sa.sql_fulltext,
    s.serial#,
    s.process,
    p.spid,
    p.tracefile
FROM v$session s,
    v$process p,
    v$sqlarea sa
WHERE s.sid =userenv('sid')--sys_context('userenv','sid')
AND s.paddr = p.addr
AND s.sql_id=sa.sql_id;
```

The output of above query contains tracefile:
```
/oracle/app/oracle/diag/rdbms/pd/trace/db_ora_12566.trc
```

Note: If the above query fails **connect** to **sys** and provide grant and then rerun the above query:
```
GRANT SELECT ON v_$session TO U1;
GRANT SELECT ON v_$process TO U1;
GRANT SELECT ON v_$sqlarea TO U1;
```

Step 4: Run the TKPROF utility (from SQL PROMPT) to convert the tracefile into human readable txt file format

SQL PROMPT>

```
ho TKPROF /oracle/app/oracle/diag/rdbms/pd/trace/db_ora_12566.trc h:\output.txt
```

Now you can open the output.txt file and do your analysis it.

If you want to see the execution plan of each query in the output.txt use this instead:

```
ho TKPROF /oracle/app/oracle/diag/rdbms/pd/trace/db_ora_12566.trc h:\output.txt
EXPLAIN=U1/U1 SYS=NO SORT=EXEELA
```

Here **U1** is username and password, SORT=EXEELA means sorting the SQL in the output.txt based on Elapsed time spent executing.

You can use different value for **SORT** parameter e.g.

EXEELA Elapsed time spent executing
PRSELA Elapsed time spent parsing
PRSDSK Number of physical reads from disk during parse
EXECNT Number of executes
FCHCNT Number of fetches

Advice 72: Fundamental of HEAT MAP in 12c

Prior to 12c Information Lifecycle Management (ILM) assistant performs archival of data from high performance storage to low cost storage.

Oracle 12c (under ILM) has introduced "heat map" and "automatic data optimization (ADO)" to improve data storage and compression.
Using heat map oracle internally either compress data or move data to low cost storage tablespace. It tracks when data is being accessed at table level and row level. Heat map provide specific information about the age of data based on hot, warm or cold as explained below:

Hot: It means data is accessed/modified frequently and last accessed/modified date is less than 2 days.
Warm: It means data is accessed/modified not so frequently and last accessed/modified date is greater than 5 days but less than 60 days.
Cold: It means data is accessed/modified rarely and last accessed/modified date is greater than 60 days.

Note: In one single table you can have all these three sets of data.

Implementation of heat map:
The "HEAT_MAP" initialization parameter is used to enable or disable heat map as well as Automatic Data Optimization (ADO). By default it is disabled (OFF).

```
ALTER session SET HEAT_MAP=ON;--session level
ALTER system SET HEAT_MAP =ON;--system level
```

Once enabled all the table and data will be tracked.

Heat map captures details (e.g. read, write, full scan, index lookup etc.) using dictionary view V$HEAT_MAP_SEGMENT and user views USER_HEAT_MAP_SEGMENT, USER_HEAT_MAP_SEQ_HISTOGRAM, USER_HEATMAP_TOP_OBJECTS.

Using heat map, oracle automates policy-driven data movement and compression. To do that DBA has to create multiple policies which compress the set of data (**hot**) in "OLTP" mode, **warm** data can be compressed using "compress for query" mode, and **cold** data can be compressed using "compress for archive" mode. Also DBA can create one more policy to move the **cold** data to low cost storage space.
These policies once created by DBA, are invoked automatically when age criteria for the data is satisfied.

Advice 73: Multitenant container database with Pluggable database option in 12c

Oracle 12c multitenant container database is based on the architecture for next generation cloud.
In this architecture there is a container database which hold many pluggable databases. All the pluggable databases share the same memory and background process of the container database.

Consider the scenario where in your organization you have a database with set of schema say HR, SALES, GIS, FIN and different group say "DEVELOPER", "TESTER", "DESIGNER" and "DBA" want to use the same framework to do certain work uninterrupted.

In order to achieve that you have to create 4 physical database which means you have to maintain 4 instances.

However in Oracle 12c by virtue of multitenant architecture you can create many pluggable databases which will share the same instance. Now same framework can be independently used by "DEVELOPER", "TESTER", "DESIGNER" and "DBA" By simply creating 4 pluggable databases.

Here are the setup:

Connect to sys as sysdba and run all the commands.

To see if 12c database has been created as CDB (container database) just run:
```
SELECT cdb FROM v$database;
```
This will return "YES" or "NO"

To see how many pluggable database are present
```
SELECT con_id, dbid, name FROM v$pdbs;
```
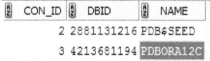

To drop a pluggable database:
```
ALTER pluggable DATABASE PDBORA12C CLOSE immediate;
DROP pluggable DATABASE PDBORA12C including datafiles;
```

Now you see how many pluggable database are present because one is dropped.
```
SELECT con_id, dbid, name FROM v$pdbs;
```
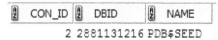

To create a pluggable database:

```
SELECT file_name FROM dba_data_files;
```

FILE_NAME
C:\APP\ASIM.A\ORADATA\ORA12C\USERS01.DBF
C:\APP\ASIM.A\ORADATA\ORA12C\UNDOTBS01.DBF
C:\APP\ASIM.A\ORADATA\ORA12C\SYSTEM01.DBF
C:\APP\ASIM.A\ORADATA\ORA12C\SYSAUX01.DBF

```
CREATE pluggable DATABASE pdb_test admin USER dbaclass IDENTIFIED BY dbaclass
FILE_NAME_CONVERT=('C:\APP\ASIM.A\ORADATA\ORA12C\PDBSEED\',
'C:\APP\ASIM.A\ORADATA\ORA12C\pdb_test\');
```

```
ALTER pluggable DATABASE pdb_test OPEN;
```

You see how many pluggable database are present
```
SELECT con_id, dbid, name FROM v$pdbs;
```

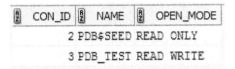

CON_ID	NAME	OPEN_MODE
2	PDB$SEED	READ ONLY
3	PDB_TEST	READ WRITE

"DEVELOPER" can use this pluggable database by running the following command:
```
ALTER session SET container=pdb_test;
```

Now he can use the common framework with set of schemas and work independently.

Similarly you can create another 3 pluggable databases for "DESIGNER", "TESTER" and "DBA"

This way each and every user can use the same framework in terms of object, schema, synonyms etc. without any hindrance by other users.

This is truly a boon for database administrator.

Advice 74: Finding refunded transaction

One interesting case study where you need to find all the transactions which was deposited and withdrawn within 5 days. Let us explain with an example:

```
CREATE TABLE txn
  (
    acc                NUMBER,
    branch             NUMBER,
    txn_date           DATE,
    Deposit_withdrwan  VARCHAR2(1),
    amt                NUMBER
  );
```

```
Insert into TXN (ACC,BRANCH,TXN_DATE,Deposit_withdrwan,AMT) values (1,1,to_date('10-02-2017 00:00:00','dd-mm-yyyy hh24:mi:ss'),'D',100);
Insert into TXN (ACC,BRANCH,TXN_DATE,Deposit_withdrwan,AMT) values (1,1,to_date('13-02-2017 00:00:00','dd-mm-yyyy hh24:mi:ss'),'D',110);
Insert into TXN (ACC,BRANCH,TXN_DATE,Deposit_withdrwan,AMT) values (1,1,to_date('15-02-2017 00:00:00','dd-mm-yyyy hh24:mi:ss'),'W',-100);
Insert into TXN (ACC,BRANCH,TXN_DATE,Deposit_withdrwan,AMT) values (1,1,to_date('10-02-2017 00:00:00','dd-mm-yyyy hh24:mi:ss'),'D',100);
Insert into TXN (ACC,BRANCH,TXN_DATE,Deposit_withdrwan,AMT) values (2,2,to_date('10-02-2017 00:00:00','dd-mm-yyyy hh24:mi:ss'),'D',200);
Insert into TXN (ACC,BRANCH,TXN_DATE,Deposit_withdrwan,AMT) values (2,2,to_date('13-02-2017 00:00:00','dd-mm-yyyy hh24:mi:ss'),'W',-200);
Insert into TXN (ACC,BRANCH,TXN_DATE,Deposit_withdrwan,AMT) values (1,1,to_date('16-02-2017 00:00:00','dd-mm-yyyy hh24:mi:ss'),'W',-110);
Insert into TXN (ACC,BRANCH,TXN_DATE,Deposit_withdrwan,AMT) values (2,2,to_date('15-02-2017 00:00:00','dd-mm-yyyy hh24:mi:ss'),'D',300);
Insert into TXN (ACC,BRANCH,TXN_DATE,Deposit_withdrwan,AMT) values (1,1,to_date('14-02-2017 00:00:00','dd-mm-yyyy hh24:mi:ss'),'W',-100);
Insert into TXN (ACC,BRANCH,TXN_DATE,Deposit_withdrwan,AMT) values (1,1,to_date('13-02-2017 00:00:00','dd-mm-yyyy hh24:mi:ss'),'D',100);
```

```
SELECT * FROM TXN ORDER BY acc,deposit_withdrwan;
```

ACC	BRANCH	TXN_DATE	DEPOSIT_WITHDRWAN	AMT
1	1	10-02-2017 00:00:00	D	100
1	1	13-02-2017 00:00:00	D	110
1	1	10-02-2017 00:00:00	D	100
1	1	13-02-2017 00:00:00	D	100
1	1	15-02-2017 00:00:00	W	-100
1	1	14-02-2017 00:00:00	W	-100
1	1	16-02-2017 00:00:00	W	-110
2	2	15-02-2017 00:00:00	D	300
2	2	10-02-2017 00:00:00	D	200
2	2	13-02-2017 00:00:00	W	-200

Now you want to get only the transaction which was deposited and subsequently withdrawn and hence need to display the output with shaded rows as below. Other rows which has only deposit but no withdrawn will not be shown in the output.

ACC	BRANCH	TXN_DATE	DEPOSIT_WITHDRWAN	AMT
1	1	10-02-2017 00:00:00	D	100
1	1	13-02-2017 00:00:00	D	110
1	1	10-02-2017 00:00:00	D	100
1	1	13-02-2017 00:00:00	D	100
1	1	15-02-2017 00:00:00	W	-100
1	1	14-02-2017 00:00:00	W	-100
1	1	16-02-2017 00:00:00	W	-110
2	2	15-02-2017 00:00:00	D	300
2	2	10-02-2017 00:00:00	D	200
2	2	13-02-2017 00:00:00	W	-200

131

Here is the solution:

```
SELECT *
FROM
  (SELECT A.*,
     row_number() over(partition BY A.acc,A.amt order by A.txn_date) AS rn
  FROM
    ( SELECT * FROM txn WHERE Deposit_withdrwan='D'
    )A
  )X,
  (SELECT *
  FROM
    (SELECT m.acc,
       m.branch,
       m.Deposit_withdrwan,
       m.amt,
       m.txn_date,
       n.ref_cnt,
       row_number() over(partition BY m.acc,m.branch,m.Deposit_withdrwan,m.amt
       order by m.txn_date)rr
    FROM txn m,
      (SELECT acc,
         branch,
         Deposit_withdrwan,
         amt,
         COUNT(*) ref_cnt
      FROM txn
      WHERE Deposit_withdrwan='W'
      GROUP BY acc,
        branch,
        Deposit_withdrwan,
        amt
      ) n
    WHERE m.Deposit_withdrwan='W'
    AND m.acc    =n.acc
    AND m.branch=n.branch
    AND m.Deposit_withdrwan  =n.Deposit_withdrwan
    AND m.amt    =n.amt
    )
  WHERE rr=1
  ) B
WHERE X.acc              =b.acc
AND X.branch             =b.branch
AND X.amt                =(B.amt)*-1
AND x.rn                 <=B.ref_cnt
AND (B.txn_date-X.txn_date)<=5;
```

The output look as below:

ACC	BRANCH	TXN_DATE	DEPOSIT_WITHDRWAN	AMT	RN	ACC_1	BRANCH_1	DEP...	AMT_1	TXN_DATE_1	REF_CNT	RR
1	1	10-02-2017 00:00:00	D	100	1	1	1	W	-100	14-02-2017 ...	2	1
1	1	10-02-2017 00:00:00	D	100	2	1	1	W	-100	14-02-2017 ...	2	1
1	1	13-02-2017 00:00:00	D	110	1	1	1	W	-110	16-02-2017 ...	1	1
2	2	10-02-2017 00:00:00	D	200	1	2	2	W	-200	13-02-2017 ...	1	1

INDEX PAGE

Query used to generate the index page:

```
SELECT upper(rpad(idx,30,'-'))
   ||page_number "Index Page"
FROM
   ( SELECT DISTINCT idx,
     listagg(page_no,',') within GROUP(
   ORDER BY page_no) over(partition BY idx) page_number
   FROM test_a
   ORDER BY 1
   )
ORDER BY 1;
```

A

B

C

H

I

J

K

L

M

S

T

U

V

W

X